COLLINS
WINNING BRIDGE

MORE BEDSIDE BRIDGE

EDITED BY ELENA JERONIMIDIS

CollinsWillow
An Imprint of HarperCollinsPublishers

First published in 1996 by
CollinsWillow
an imprint of HarperCollins*Publishers*
London

© Elena Jeronimidis 1996

1 3 5 7 9 8 6 4 2

A CIP catalogue record for this book
is available from the British Library

ISBN 0 00 218764 7

Printed and bound in Great Britain by
Caledonian International Book Manufacturing Ltd, Glasgow

Text snippets and cartoons in tinted boxes
(the latter originally sponsored by *Carta Mundi*)
reproduced by permission of *Bridge Plus*
p 16: Excerpt from *Farewell, my Dummy!*
printed by permission of Batsford publishers
p 144: Excerpt from *Garozzo's Corner*
reprinted by permission of *Bridge d'Italia*
pp 151 and 174: Quiz from *The 1997 Daily Bridge Calendar*
reprinted by permission of the publishers Copp Clark Limited
p 186: Article reprinted by permission of
International Popular Bridge Monthly

CONTENTS

It Happened One Night (continued)

Better Bridge 99

Bridge-à-brac 147

Bridge-à-brac (continued)

Tournament Bridge

Who's Who

ACKNOWLEDGEMENTS

This book is very much the result of a collective effort, and I am grateful to all the writers for their enthusiastic cooperation — which, most unusually, extended to respecting my deadlines.

I also wish to thank Eric Crowhurst and Roger Trowell for reading the manuscript; Sally Brock and Tony Gordon for much constructive criticism; and Andrew Parker for assistance whenever needed.

Elena Jeronimidis, 1996

INTRODUCTION

BY ELENA JERONIMIDIS

It is estimated that there are some three million bridge players in the UK. Trying to guess how many there are on our planet Earth is mind-boggling.

The articles contained in *More Bedside Bridge* come from all over the world, and show how much bridge is loved by its aficionados — irrespective of nationality and standard of play. It is indeed a characteristic of the game that it can be enjoyed at all levels: the satisfaction of a successful play or defence often has little to do with technical complexity — just as compatibility, rather than card skills, is often what we look for in our partners.

Although it has now gained international recognition as a sport, bridge is still primarily a social game whose practitioners rate congenial company higher than Olympic medals. Yet by its very nature bridge also fosters competitiveness, so that it is not unusual to find a pecking order even in the lowliest foursome of rank beginners. Whether this is because bridge is a battle of wits, or because, being a partnership game, it reflects the battle for supremacy inherent in human interaction, is for you to decide.

Contributors to *More Bedside Bridge* sit on all rungs of the world's bridge ladder — though perhaps, in comparison with the earlier *Bedside Book of Bridge*, the number of those who play top-class bridge is higher. The choice of articles reflects the variety of interests, experience, and expertise of authors and readers alike, the resulting collection not just containing useful advice backed up by success at the table, but also portraying the whole range of emotions that all bridge players experience: from frustration to amusement, and from disappointment to elation.

For the reader's convenience, this book is divided into sections ('Bridge Fiction', 'It Happened One Night', 'Better Bridge', 'Bridge-à-brac' and 'Tournament Bridge'), each described on the relevant introductory page. Which one will be your favourite will depend on your taste — but in all of them you will find reflected that maddening element of unpredictability that represents the main fascination of bridge.

BRIDGE FICTION

*B*ridge is a game which, above all others, exercises the mind and stimulates the imagination. The pages that follow show that a bridge-player's imagination knows no bounds — of time, place, audacity … and shame!

THE ABBOT'S CARELESS OPENING LEAD

BY DAVID BIRD

With little prospect of a £1 game, the Abbot had joined the 10p table, much to the alarm of its other occupants. He raised a despairing eyebrow as he cut Brother Aelred as partner. Still, he thought, 10p players were all as weak as each other.

The first rubber had climbed to Game All when this deal arose:

Dealer: North
Game All

Brother Stephen
♠ 9 7 2
♡ A K Q 8 4
◇ J 9 2
♣ 6 3

The Abbot
♠ K Q J 10 4
♡ J 10 6 3
◇ A 4
♣ 9 7

Brother Aelred
♠ 6 3
♡ 9 7 5
◇ K Q 8 7 6 3
♣ 5 4

```
      N
  W       E
      S
```

Brother Zac
♠ A 8 5
♡ 2
◇ 10 5
♣ A K Q J 10 8 2

South	West	North	East
		1♡	NB
3♣	NB	3♡	NB
4NT	NB	5◇	NB
6♣	End		

The Abbot led the ♠K and the young novice sitting North displayed his dummy.

'Good gracious!' exclaimed the Abbot. 'Don't tell me that counts as a vulnerable opening bid nowadays.'

'It was rather awkward, Abbot,' replied the angelic Brother Stephen. 'I would have opened a weak two at duplicate but, with only a five-card suit, I wasn't sure if it was allowed at rubber bridge.'

'I suppose the possibility of passing never occurred to you?' said the Abbot heavily.

'Well, I was reading an old book by Culbertson this afternoon,' replied the novice. 'It said that you should open the bidding if you hold one-and-a-half honour tricks.'

The Abbot gave a pained sigh. 'Culbertson's mark was two-and-a-half honour tricks,' he said. 'Not one-and-a-half.'

The black-bearded Brother Zac won the spade lead in the South hand. He had escaped a diamond lead, but how many top tricks did he have? Seven clubs, three hearts and one spade. What bad luck, only eleven. The best hope seemed to be to run the clubs, hoping that someone would throw a heart away. Brother Aelred threw the wrong thing away more often than not. Still, with dummy's heart holding exposed on the table, it was a bit much to expect, even from him.

When the club suit was run it was the Abbot, sitting West, who came under pressure. He could release one diamond and three spades without any problem, but this was the position with one club still to go:

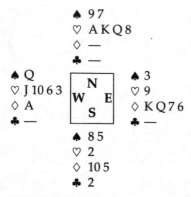

On the last club the Abbot could scarcely bear to part with a card. A major-suit discard would obviously give declarer a twelfth trick, so he had to throw the ◇ A.

If South had the ◇ K, as seemed likely, that card would squeeze him a second time and an overtrick would result.

'I dare say I should have led this card,' declared the Abbot loudly, tossing the ◇ A on to the table. 'You would still make twelve but at least I'd prevent the repeating squeeze.'

Brother Zac, who was not in fact blessed with the ◇ K, now had to judge what to throw from the dummy. It seemed clear from the

14

Abbot's sequence of discards that he still held a heart guard. Brother Zac therefore threw a heart from dummy on the last club. Holding his breath, he then led a spade towards dummy's ♠9. The Abbot won with the ♠Q and, somewhat gracelessly, had to concede the remaining tricks to the dummy. The slam had been made.

'I had the king-queen of diamonds, Abbot,' declared Brother Aelred. 'If you lead the ace I can give you a come-on signal and you can play another diamond. That's one down, isn't it?'

The Abbot, not greatly amused at having his defence criticised by the weakest player in the monastery, glared across the table. 'With king-queen-jack of spades and an ace, you wouldn't lead a spade?' he demanded.

'No, I always lead an ace against a slam,' replied Brother Aelred. 'It's a lesson I've learnt from bitter experience.'

'Table up!' called Brother Zac, pocketing his winnings on the rubber.

No-one was eager to join a table including the Abbot, so the same four cut once more for partners. This time the draw put Brother Aelred and Brother Zac together.

'Weak no-trump and take-out doubles of three bids, partner?' queried Brother Aelred.

Brother Zac nodded.

'Ace from ace-king?' continued Brother Aelred. 'Oh yes, and if you don't mind, always lead an ace against a slam.'

PRIDE AND PREJUDICE

BY PHILLIP AND ROBERT KING

It is a truth universally acknowledged that a single man in possession of a life mastership must be in want of a bridge partner. It was this prejudice which persuaded Miss Elizabeth Bennet to take seats behind Mr Darcy.

He was a tall, proud man. His handsome features, and the report of his having ten thousand a year, had attracted a regiment of eligible young ladies, which his disagreeable manners had swiftly reduced to a mere battalion.

In the first rubber, he partnered his devoted admirer, Miss Bingley, and this pair seemed more than a match for their opponents. The modest Mr Bingley invariably expected to lose, and was seldom disappointed; while Elizabeth's flirtatious sister, Lydia, joyously distracted by a close circle of amorous militia officers, could scarcely tell a knave from a king.

Elizabeth, whose greatest pleasure was to laugh at human folly, soon found much to amuse her.

'We play a natural system,' Mr Darcy announced. 'For although I hold that convention is the basis of civilised society, I regard conventions as vile perversions of truth.'

'Come, Darcy,' said Bingley. 'Some of them are very useful.'

'To those who prize artificiality above sincerity, perhaps,' his friend replied. 'When my partner opens a no-trump, my two club response is a promise that I have clubs, not a clandestine attempt to discover length in the major suits.'

Having demolished one convention, he seemed bent on the destruction of all the others, until Mr Bingley hurriedly completed the first deal and passed with unseemly haste:

Dealer: West
Love All

Miss Bingley
♠ K 10 8 5 2
♡ A 10
♢ Q 9 6
♣ A J 4

Mr Bingley
♠ 6 3
♡ J 8 5 4 2
♢ 4 3
♣ 10 9 6 2

```
      N
  W       E
      S
```

Miss Lydia Bennet
♠ A J 9 7
♡ K Q 9 7 6 3
♢ 7
♣ K 8

Mr Darcy
♠ Q 4
♡ —
♢ A K J 10 8 5 2
♣ Q 7 5 3

South	West	North	East
	NB	1♠	2♡
5♢	NB	6♢	End

Let other pens dwell on the vulgarity of the auction; mine will dwell on the poverty of the dummy play.

Winning the heart lead on the table, Mr Darcy discarded a club, and ruffed the remaining heart. With a masterful air, he drew trumps, and a concerted gasp of feminine admiration, then called for a spade from the table.

Lydia withdrew her hand from a blushing young lieutenant's just in time to play a random ♠7 in tempo, and declarer won with the queen. Capturing the next round of spades with the ♠9, she carelessly returned a heart to the table, and her hand to the lieutenant. Although this allowed Mr Darcy to discard a club, while ruffing in dummy, it proved to be of no advantage to him.

A third spade was ruffed in the closed hand, but when Mr Bingley shewed out, with a profuse apology, Mr Darcy looked grave. Lacking sufficient entries to set up the suit, he was compelled to hazard the club finesse. Lydia, with an ill-bred squeal of delight, produced the king, bringing a flush of shame from Elizabeth, and an end to declarer's slam ambitions.

'What wretched fortune, Mr Darcy,' observed Miss Bingley. 'But for the cruel disposition of the black suits, your accomplished dummy play would have been justly rewarded.'

'Possibly,' he replied. 'Yet I am by no means persuaded that I managed the hand in a manner befitting my rank.'

Elizabeth could not resist a sly smile. 'Your modesty is to be commended, Sir,' she teased him, 'particularly as in this instance you have much to be modest about.'

'Perhaps I should have essayed a spade from dummy at trick two,' he murmured, gazing into her fine dark eyes.

'Perhaps,' she gazed back at him, 'but you would still have lost the setting trick to the club king.'

'Admit defeat, Miss Bennet,' Miss Bingley cried triumphantly. 'The contract was foredoomed.'

'Your admonition places me in a quandary, Miss Bingley,' said Elizabeth, cleverly apprehending that Darcy preferred her own daring impertinence to the obsequious attentions of his partner. 'To admit defeat might improve Mr Darcy's temper; to deny it might improve his card sense.'

'Then deny it, by all means,' cried Mr Darcy with passion, 'for no man of sensibility should miss an opportunity to profit from sensible instruction.'

'I fear that your play to the opening lead was precipitate,' said Elizabeth, pressing for victory. 'I would have ruffed in hand. Then, after drawing trumps, I would advance a low spade from the table, placing my sister in a most improper position.'

When this remark exacted a lewd peal of laughter from Lydia, and a disdainful curl of the lip from Miss Bingley, she hastily continued: 'If Lydia plays low, I will win, enter dummy with the ♣A, and discard a spade on the ♡A.'

'Which you preserved with great cunning,' sneered Miss Bingley. 'But your sister will surely capture the first spade, particularly with half a platoon to advise her.'

'Then I would be able to establish three spade winners,' said Elizabeth. 'And these, together with my *cunningly* preserved ♡A, would allow me to discard three losing clubs, and all this without the benefit of military intelligence.'

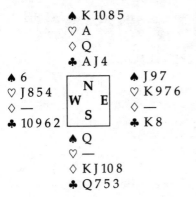

```
        ♠ K 10 8 5
        ♡ A
        ◇ Q
        ♣ A J 4
♠ 6              ♠ J 9 7
♡ J 8 5 4        ♡ K 9 7 6
◇ —              ◇ —
♣ 10 9 6 2       ♣ K 8
        ♠ Q
        ♡ —
        ◇ K J 10 8
        ♣ Q 7 5 3
```

'Darcy, I do believe Miss Bennet is correct,' cried Mr Bingley, nobly breaking the awkward silence.

'If so, I may claim no credit,' said Elizabeth. 'In advocating the principle of forcing a victim to choose between two unattractive alternatives, I was surely anticipated by Cardinal Morton.'

'Morton's fork!' exclaimed Mr Darcy, his eyes smouldering. 'That grasping chancellor taxed those whose handsome way of life manifested their opulence; or the miserly, who must have grown rich by their economy. My ancestors were his principal sufferers, to the monstrous tune of a shilling in the pound.'

Elizabeth rapidly deducted one from twenty, and, discovering the remainder to be nineteen, regarded him with quickening interest. The sole heir to the kingdom's foremost taxpayers might readily be forgiven for his cold manner, perhaps even for his butchery of cold contracts. He had also shewn a surprising tolerance of wholesome criticism, a physic which she loved to administer in large doses.

THE QUALITY OF EVIL

BY GUSTAVU AGLIONE

'Felix?' I feel ridiculous. Being Father Christmas is one thing, but to wear a Santa Claus outfit? And to yell 'Ho-ho' all the time? No, that's not my piece of Christmas Pudding.

'I thought your first name was Felix?'

I repeat my question to the sinister-looking gentleman on my right, who has introduced himself politely as Dzamoludine Dzerzhinski.

He laughs at me and says: 'No, Felix is my younger brother. A very soft type who founded KGB. It is absolutely right that the *hoi polloi* removed his statue opposite Lubianka Prison. Only genuine Evil deserves such a monument in Moscow!'

Well, one can have a different opinion about this. It is a strange situation anyway. I am dressed as Santa Claus and I am sitting at a bridge table with the obligation to shout 'Ho-ho' once in a while. We are playing only one hand in a Par contest, and we have the obligation to win that hand. Why?

Well, Galina and I are representing Good and our redoubtable opponents are the personification of Evil. On my left-hand side is the God of War — Mars, Ares, or whatever name he is known by in all parts of the world — and his partner is Dzamoludine Dzerzhinski, whom I seem to know but who is apparently worse than his naive baby brother.

We play just one hand. And if we win by beating par, Evil will postpone its reign for just another year. Why did people choose me? I am not a good bridge-player. No, it must be a dream. It has to be — for Galina, who is sitting opposite me, is looking lovelier than ever in her disguise as one of Santa's Elves.

I am North, and this is my hand:

♠ A K Q 8 2
♡ A 7 4
♢ 10 9 4 3 2
♣ —

It is Game All and Galina is first to speak: 'Three no-trump,' she says.

This indicates A-K-Q-x-x-x-x in a minor with almost nothing extra. Well, I know which minor it is!

West bids 4♣.

Did I really know Galina's minor? I thought it to be clubs, but with my holding she could equally well have A-K-Q-x-x-x-x in diamonds. Well, that is wonderful, since with seven tricks in diamonds together with two club ruffs and ♠A-K-Q and the ♡A I can count thirteen tricks.

'Seven diamonds,' I bid very confidently.

This, however, is not the end of the auction, which proceeds:

South	West	North	East
Galina	*Dzerzhinski*	*Gustavu*	*Mars*
3NT	4♣	7◇	NB
NB	Dbl	Redbl	NB
7♡	Dbl	NB	NB
7♠	Dbl	Redbl	End

Well, of course there was something going on, and apparently only Galina had smelled the rat after Dz.Dz.'s double of 7◇ and my redouble. She sensed the nature of Dz.Dz.'s 4♣ bid, and somehow felt that he'd laid a trap. Therefore she corrected to 7♡ and, when I failed to redouble this contract, tried 7♠ in a final attempt to find the better major.

So now we are in 7♠ redoubled to be played by Galina as South:

♠ A K Q 8 2
♡ A 7 4
◇ 10 9 4 3 2
♣ —

```
    N
 W     E
    S
```

♠ J 5 4
♡ 9 8 3
◇ —
♣ A K Q 10 8 7 3

West leads the ◇A, ruffed by South. Do you see thirteen tricks?

It takes Galina ten seconds to spot the solution: the ◇A ruffed is followed by the ♣A-K under which West plays the ♣J, while hearts are discarded from dummy. The ♣Q is not ruffed by West, nor the ♣10: West discards hearts and dummy diamonds.

Now Galina cashes the ♡A in dummy, ruffs a diamond with the ♠5, ruffs a heart in dummy with the ♠2, the last diamond with her ♠J, the last heart with the ♠8, and claims thirteen tricks. This is the full deal:

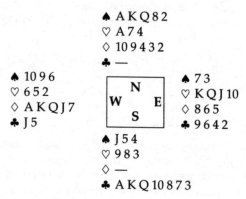

Ho-ho! This is incredible! Certainly above par, since 7♠ redoubled vulnerable is good for 2940 points. Galina, too, is very much aware of that — her elfish happiness is transparent.

Mars in the meantime is trying to choke Dz.Dz. 'You stupid blockhead!' he shouts. 'Why don't you just pass the 7◇ bid? The double is unnecessary, since by beating 7◇ we beat par anyway!'

Galina smiles: 'Yes, I smelled a rat — fortunately, in time,' she says. 'That 4♣, by the way, is a great psychological bid. We should try to remember it! As for the rest, in 7♠ I just need the black suits to break as they do, plus, of course, three hearts with West, because I can cash the ♡A only after taking four discards on the top four clubs. After trick four West is the victim of an Agony Squeeze, and at trick seven he is caught in a cross-ruff. Had the ♠7 and ♠8 been interchanged, he would have been able to give dummy a double uppercut by ruffing the ♣Q and ♣10 with the ♠9 and ♠10 — but on the lie of the cards, there was no way for him to save the day.'

Save *their* day, of course — and lead to *our* doomsday! We are eternally lucky that Evil can be so stupid in its greed ... Ho-ho!

PRICELESS PLAY

BY QUEENIE PENGUIN

The small group of regulars lingering at the bar were all agog with curiosity. News that a major sponsor was seeking to hire a bridge partner had reached even the sheltered icebergs of South Georgia, so that the sudden appearance of Icicle P. Cubes at the *Emperor's* duplicate session had given rise to a lot of speculation.

'Mind you,' twittered Lina Macaroni, sipping her gin and tonic, 'I don't see why he should need to pay to get a partner. They say he's a very good player himself — and he's very good-looking!'

'That,' said Colonel Chinstrap jovially, 'is a circumstance which might impress a pretty young female like you, but I opine it would not be a determining factor in winning Antarctic Championships!'

'On the other hand,' mused the Jackass, who that evening had had the dubious privilege of partnering the Little Blue Penguin, 'he has such charming manners that it's difficult to imagine anyone refusing to play with him. I agree with Miss Macaroni: both as a penguin and as a player, one cannot see why he needs to pay to play, so to speak.'

'It is often the best players,' offered Elspeth, 'who hire their partners. I have heard it said that they do so in order to get a better game.'

'Yeah, and I have heard it said that they do so to make sure partner never criticises them,' mimicked the Little Blue Penguin. 'Be your age, sister: if you hire your partner and team-mates like this Cube dude does, it's because you've got money to throw away and you wanna win at all costs. Not that I blame him for that,' added Little Blue reflectively. 'If I had the money, I wouldn't mind hiring me a few top players and going around winning events. I guess the next-best thing for me would be to get myself hired, but the dude said nothing to me — or to anyone else for that matter.'

'Not quite!' cried the Gentoo merrily, as he entered the room together with his partner. 'If someone buys me and Archibald a drink, I'll tell you the story.'

Two pints having appeared at the speed of light, the Gentoo settled down to scribble a diagram on a beer mat:

Dealer: East
E/W Vul.

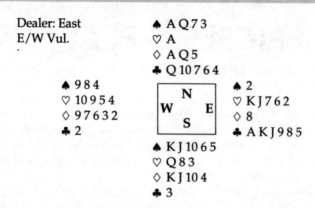

♠ A Q 7 3
♡ A
◇ A Q 5
♣ Q 10 7 6 4

♠ 9 8 4
♡ 10 9 5 4
◇ 9 7 6 3 2
♣ 2

♠ 2
♡ K J 7 6 2
◇ 8
♣ A K J 9 8 5

♠ K J 10 6 5
♡ Q 8 3
◇ K J 10 4
♣ 3

'I know the hand!' cried Little Blue. 'I was South; the bidding went:

South	West	North	East
			1♣
1♠	NB	2♣*	2♡
NB	3♡	4♡	5♡
6♠	End		
*Forcing			

'West led the ♣2 and East, after winning trick one, continued with the ♣A. On the bidding I was pretty sure that East had five hearts and six clubs, though I had no way of guessing his holding in spades and diamonds. Whatever his shape, though, I could see twelve tricks if I ruffed two hearts in dummy so, minding my entries as well as the possibility that East had two spades and a diamond void, I ruffed trick two with the ♠10, West discarding the ◇2. Then I played the ♠5 to the ♠A, cashed the ♡A, and came back to hand with the ♠J, East throwing a club. The rest was easy: I next ruffed a heart with ♠7, came back to hand with the ◇10, ruffed my last heart with the ♠Q, cashed the ◇A, crossed to hand with the ◇Q to ◇K, drew the last trump and made the ◇J as my twelfth trick. What's so difficult about the hand?' concluded Little Blue.

'You timed the play nicely,' drawled Archibald graciously.

'Well, wouldn't anyone?' asked Little Blue. 'Anyone who can play, that is?'

'Ah!' exclaimed the Gentoo with a twinkle in his merry eyes. 'But Archibald was playing against Mr Cubes, on the last round of the evening, and decided to set himself a challenge. The bidding and play to the first two tricks were the same but Archibald decided the contract would be easy if spades broke 2-2. So after ruffing trick two with the ♠10, he cashed the ♠J and ♠A. On discovering the bad news, he then proceeded to cash four rounds of diamonds, finally crossing to dummy with the ♡A to reach this position:

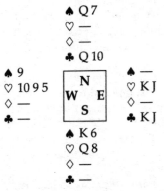

```
              ♠ Q 7
              ♡ —
              ◇ —
              ♣ Q 10
♠ 9                          ♠ —
♡ 10 9 5    ┌─────────┐      ♡ K J
◇ —         │   N     │      ◇ —
♣ —         │ W   E   │      ♣ K J
            │   S     │
            └─────────┘
              ♠ K 6
              ♡ Q 8
              ◇ —
              ♣ —
```

'When the ♠Q was played, Mr Cubes, East, was helpless. Had he dropped the ♣J, South would have played the ♠6 and set up the ♣Q with a ruff.

'In the event, Mr Cubes threw the ♡J, hoping that West held the ♡Q, but Archibald overtook the ♠Q with his ♠K, ruffed a heart in dummy felling the king, came back to hand with a club ruff and scored the last trick with his ♡Q.'

'Oh, Archie!' sighed Lina, even though she had followed neither of the two lines of play. 'Mr Cubes must have been ever so impressed. Did he ask you to play with him?'

'He was going to,' laughed the Gentoo before Archibald had a chance to speak, 'but he was not given the chance. By the time Archibald had finished telling him in the greatest detail how he had caught him in a trump squeeze *en passant*, all Mr Cubes wanted to do was leave in a hurry.'

'That's rather unlike you,' said Elspeth giving Archibald a puzzled look. 'Vain as you are, it must be admitted that you don't usually show off like that. Why did you do it?'

'I merely wanted to make sure that Mr Cubes appreciated the excellence of my play,' replied the stately penguin with studied nonchalance. 'It won't do him any harm to realise that money can't buy everything.'

THE 'FUN' EVENING

BY HILARY QUINTANA

The Mother- and Father-in-law play about once a week at a partnership rubber bridge club. Although the Husband and I are no longer members of a club, we accepted their invitation to play in a once-a-year 'Fun Evening' at theirs.

Each pair played half an hour of rubber bridge against each of six other pairs. Any deal on which at least one call had been made when the half hour was announced would be allowed to be played out. Scoring was on rubber bridge lines, but only the plus scores counted: the winning pair would take their actual score whilst the losing pair would score zero. The highest aggregate total over the six rounds would be the winner.

The Husband was quick to realise that the special scoring rules called for unusual tactics, aimed at boosting scores and increasing the number of deals played in each round. Pass out borderline hands; claim rather than play for overtricks; concede rather than defend against overtricks; double when behind anyway; and bid up. As well as reminding me of these points with increasing frequency leading up to the competition, he also insisted that we review our slam bidding after Acol Two openers. I wondered if he wasn't perhaps taking the whole thing a bit too seriously!

On the night, we were made overwhelmingly welcome. Apart from one forty-year-old partnering his father, we were the youngest players in the room. Everyone took care to introduce themselves. Those who knew us asked whether we were still playing much bridge, how the Daughter was getting on at University and the Son with his A-levels. I could see the Husband getting increasingly irritated at this waste of valuable seconds of playing time.

We began against the Mother- and Father-in-law. I dealt the first hand and we bid 1♡ — 3NT on a flat 16 opposite a flat 14. Following his own guidelines, the Husband claimed nine tricks at trick one. As we had ten tricks on top, with possibilities of a second overtrick, our surprised opponents accepted the claim.

On the next deal, the Mother-in-law played in 3NT after bidding 1NT — 3NT. The Husband led the ♣A, and this is what he could see:

Dealer: South
E/W Vul.

♠ K J 8
♡ A Q 10
◇ A J 6 3
♣ Q J 9

♠ Q 7 4
♡ 6 3
◇ 9 5
♣ A K 8 5 4 2

```
      N
  W       E
      S
```

The Husband quickly realised that there was no hope for the defence, cashed his ♣K and 'cleverly' switched to the ♠Q. Even the Mother-in-law could see that she now had twelve of the remaining eleven tricks, and managed to claim the rest, not forgetting to point out to the Husband how he had picked up the spade suit for her.

The third and fourth deals left our opponents at Game and 90. On the fifth deal, the Father-in-law opened 1NT fourth in hand. When this was passed back to the Husband, he doubled. Without waiting for her turn, the Mother-in-law demanded to know what was meant by a double after an original pass. Rather than admit that he was going for broke as we would have lost the rubber anyway, I said that it was for penalties, and indicated a maximum for his original pass. After much tut-tutting, the Mother-in-law eventually had to display her 3-count as dummy. The Husband and I each had a 12-point hand and collected 500 for two off.

As the two-minute warning had already been called, the Husband was itching to get in one final hand. Rather rudely, he urged us to hurry, and passed the cards across for me to cut. The Father-in-law reminded him that it was supposed to be a *fun* evening. On this final hand we made 4♠, giving us a first-round total of +970.

Nothing exciting happened against the second pair; we just lost an incomplete rubber, giving us a zero score for the round.

The third round was against the club Chairman. After about twenty-five minutes we were at Game All. It was the Chairman's deal and the hand was passed out.

'I only had seven points,' said the Chairman.

'And I only had nine,' replied the Chairman's Spouse.

They would not let us off the hook. The Husband had to own up that he had passed a 13-count in second position, putting his foot further into it by saying that we needed a good round to stay in contention and that a part-score would not help much. The Chairman's Spouse leaned across the table and pointedly asked his wife to confirm that the leaflet had indicated it to be a *fun* evening. This subtlety was wasted on the Husband, but I was beginning to get the picture: our competitive approach was not appreciated.

The Husband's deal would probably be the last hand of the round. He gave some thought to passing the South hand below, before eventually making the normal opening bid of 1♡.

Whilst the Chairman's Spouse was considering doubling, spading, or passing, the two-minute warning was called and an announcement was made that there would be no formal break but dummy should collect teas, coffees and biscuits for the table. After the interruption, West passed and I raised to 2♡. East passed, and about a minute later the Husband bid 7♡. This could not simply be a ploy to force me to fetch the drinks (any number of hearts would have done for that purpose) so I only became alarmed when, answering West's enquiry, the Husband explained that my 2♡ bid was an Acol Two showing eight playing tricks in hearts. Obviously he had forgotten that he had opened as dealer! The Chairman's Spouse doubled smartly. I remembered the laws about disregarding unauthorised information and, with a maximum for my 2♡ raise, I felt obliged to do the ethical thing: I redoubled.

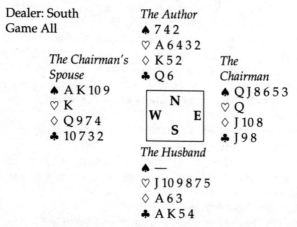

Dealer: South
Game All

The Author
♠ 7 4 2
♡ A 6 4 3 2
◇ K 5 2
♣ Q 6

The Chairman's Spouse
♠ A K 10 9
♡ K
◇ Q 9 7 4
♣ 10 7 3 2

The Chairman
♠ Q J 8 6 5 3
♡ Q
◇ J 10 8
♣ J 9 8

The Husband
♠ —
♡ J 10 9 8 7 5
◇ A 6 3
♣ A K 5 4

When I returned with the drinks, the opponents were gone, the cards were strewn across the table, and +2920 had been scrawled across my scorecard. This gave us a running total of +3890.

For the fourth round we moved to play against two Grandmothers who seemed to regard the bridge as a bit of a distraction from their conversation. They greeted us effusively and several unnecessary seconds were wasted in starting the rubber. Chatter about the weather, geraniums and the price of greeting cards continued throughout and they seemed to pay little attention to the play.

On the first two deals, they went off in a cold game and a solid part-score. They did not quite achieve the hat-trick: with eleven top tricks, they scraped home in 3NT on the third deal. We made 4♠ on the next deal, and then I dealt this hand while the opponents were flapping about with pictures of their grandchildren:

Dealer: South
Game All

The Husband
♠ K J 10
♡ A Q J
◊ K Q 7
♣ K Q 6 3

L.H. Granny
♠ 9 7 3
♡ 8 3
◊ J 10 6 2
♣ 10 9 8 4

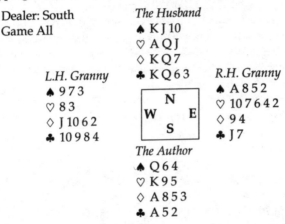

R.H. Granny
♠ A 8 5 2
♡ 10 7 6 4 2
◊ 9 4
♣ J 7

The Author
♠ Q 6 4
♡ K 9 5
◊ A 8 5 3
♣ A 5 2

The bidding proceeded: 1NT from me (12-14); 6NT from the Husband. Left-hand Granny (LHG) led the ♣10.

There were eleven tricks on top; twelve if either minor broke 3-3 or if either opponent could be squeezed in the minors. After three rounds of spades and three rounds of hearts, neither defender would be able to hold four cards in each minor. I took the ♣K and led the ♠K followed by the ♠J. To my surprise, the ♠A was held up: good defence, leaving me unable to rectify the count safely for the squeeze. I could have played a third round of spades, hoping that the defender with the ♠A started with only ♠A-x-x, but it seemed a better chance just to cash the A-K-Qs and hope for a good break in either minor. LHG won with the ◊J at trick twelve, and led the ♣9, seemingly unaware that it was a winner.

At this point, RHG realised she had no card left to play to the final trick. A search revealed her ♠A lying under a photograph album on a side table.

'I'm very sorry, partner,' she said. 'Fancy losing an ace! They would have been two off if I'd played it earlier!'

There wasn't time for another deal. We had 'won' the rubber by a magnificent +20!

We lost the fifth round, giving us a running total of +3910 going into the final round, where we found ourselves playing against two smartly dressed seventy-year-olds who introduced themselves as Major Sam Smith and Major John Jones. They were the only other pair who seemed aware of the special tactics required to win the event, and they started the round 130 ahead of us.

We managed ten deals in the thirty minutes allowed: four were passed out without comment and the rest played in game or slam. The first three complete deals were 3NT plus one by them, 4♠ doubled minus one by us, and 4♡ plus two by them, putting the Majors 1110 ahead on the round.

The next deal was ours:

Dealer: South
Love All

The Husband
♠ A 5
♡ 6 2
◇ Q 8 6 2
♣ A Q 7 6 5

Major Smith
♠ Q J 8 4
♡ J 10 9 7
◇ —
♣ K J 9 4 3

```
      N
   W     E
      S
```

Major Jones
♠ 9 6 3 2
♡ 8 5 3
◇ J 10 9 5 3
♣ 10

The Author
♠ K 10 7
♡ A K Q 4
◇ A K 7 4
♣ 8 2

South	West	North	East
1◇	Dbl	2♣	NB
3NT	NB	4◇	NB
6◇	NB	NB	Dbl
6NT	NB	NB	Dbl
End			

30

After Major Smith's fearless take-out double, Major Jones had no hesitation in doubling our 6♢ contract so loudly that most of the room turned round to look. I ran to 6NT which was also doubled — but not so loudly. The ♡J was led.

With only ten top tricks (assuming West had the ♣K and diamonds were not 3-2) the only chance seemed to be to find clubs breaking 3-3 (or possibly a defensive error coupled with a squeeze).

I took the ♡A and ducked a club to East, who played another heart. It seemed a good idea to cash a few diamonds to see if anything turned up. On the ♢A-K, West threw a spade and a club, but on the third diamond he paused. A further club discard would give away two tricks, whilst a major-suit discard would give only one trick directly but would set up a simple squeeze against his remaining two suits. Eventually he let go a heart. I took the ♠A, ♠K, and ♡Q. On the lead of the winning ♡4, West was squeezed again in the black suits.

'A repeating squeeze if I'm not mistaken. Well played, young lady,' said Major Smith — a charming gentleman.

The Majors made 3NT plus one on the next deal, but we completed the rubber with 4♠ just making. We won the round by +310.

'If we hadn't doubled you in 6NT, we would still have lost the round, but would have finished just ahead of you overall,' said Major Jones.

The Husband, who had been remarkably well behaved since half-time, couldn't resist replying, 'And maybe a few more pairs would have finished ahead of us if you hadn't doubled 6♢!'

After a few minutes, the Chairman announced the results, remarking on the unexpectedly low scores, and congratulating the winners through gritted teeth. We had finished with the highest score, just ahead of the Majors, and claimed our bottle prizes.

While we were helping to stack away the chairs, I saw the Chairman's Spouse take the Father-in-law to one side, talking animatedly and looking over towards us occasionally. I don't think that we will be invited back next year to defend our title (but I wonder if I could get the Majors' phone numbers).

THE BRIDGE CLUB MYSTERY

BY PETER DUNN
with apologies to A.C. Doyle

Holmes and Watson were relaxing at home one Thursday evening. Holmes was busy doing a crossword puzzle while Watson watched a recording of 'The Bill'.

'I need a ten-letter word ending in Y,' said Holmes.

'Elementary?'

'No, it's something to do with food,' he mused.

Suddenly, there was a knock on the door. 'Who can that be?' asked Watson, pleased to be relieved of the strain of thinking.

'Probably the police,' replied Holmes. 'They were here three Wednesdays ago with a mystery, and there's usually a major crime committed every two or three weeks, so they're overdue.' Watson opened the door to reveal the figure of Police Inspector Waxworth.

'Good evening, Inspector,' Holmes greeted him . 'Who has been killed at the Baker Street Bridge Club?'

'How did you know that?' asked Waxworth.

'Well, you're clutching what looks like the remains of a pint of bitter, and the bridge club is the only place around here where you can get it at prices *you* can afford. Besides, Thursday night is when the players take it seriously. It must mean a murder there.'

'By Gad, Holmes, you're incredible. Their star player, Mad Jimmy Baskerville, has been stabbed. His partner, Fat Andy Moriarty, has disappeared.'

The trio made their way to the bridge club. 'Apparently they were sitting North-South, and the last board had just been played,' said the Inspector, 'when Baskerville and Moriarty went downstairs. Baskerville was later found stabbed in the lavatory, and nobody knows where Moriarty went. He's not returned home.'

Holmes examined the body of Mad Jimmy, then asked to see the hands which had been played. He was taken to the table which still had the boards on it. He took out the following cards:

Dealer: North
Love All

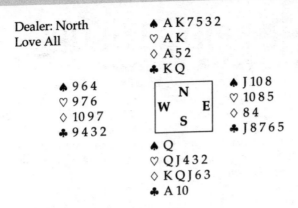

♠ A K 7 5 3 2
♡ A K
◇ A 5 2
♣ K Q

♠ 9 6 4
♡ 9 7 6
◇ 10 9 7
♣ 9 4 3 2

♠ J 10 8
♡ 10 8 5
◇ 8 4
♣ J 8 7 6 5

♠ Q
♡ Q J 4 3 2
◇ K Q J 6 3
♣ A 10

'What a hand!' exclaimed Watson. 'There don't seem to be any losers. Let's see, there's a grand slam in hearts, spades, diamonds, or no-trumps! I wonder what they were in?'

The traveller was produced, but the contract had not been filled in. 'It's been scored as +920: a bottom,' said Holmes.

'Why, that's only 6◇ without an overtrick! No wonder Moriarty stabbed him: anybody would do the same.'

'You're wrong there, Watson,' said Holmes, lighting his pipe. 'Andy Moriarty was the declarer, not Baskerville. The corpse only had a black pen in his pocket, but the traveller's written in blue, so he wasn't sitting North. Moriarty must have opened with a bid of 2♣, and after a positive response they had trouble agreeing a suit. Eventually Baskerville probably cue-bid 5♣ to show his ace and Moriarty replied 6♣ showing the king and hoping to get into a grand slam. Baskerville now got confused and assumed the club bid was genuine and passed, only having a doubleton and preferring it to Moriarty's spades. In 6◇ everybody makes thirteen tricks without thinking, so that couldn't have been the contract.'

'But how do you make 6♣, Holmes?'

'Any lead except a trump should do it. Say a spade is led to the queen; take the ♡A-K, ♠A-K, ◇A-K, and ♡Q throwing a diamond. That's eight tricks, then you cross-ruff four more.'

'Amazing, Holmes.'

'Not at all. You just follow the adage of taking your side-suit winners before embarking on a cross-ruff.'

'So all we need do now is arrest Moriarty, who must have been mad at being left in it.'

'No, of course not. He did his best making twelve tricks. Besides, what a wonderful hand to show to your friends! He could be proud of himself despite getting a bottom. Baskerville must have been devastated at his error and committed suicide after Moriarty left.'

The others stared at him, amazed, 'So where has Moriarty gone?'

'The clue, gentlemen, is in his nickname, Fat Andy. You don't get called that by being on a diet, and they don't serve food here. He'll be in the nearest restaurant putting something in the canal.'

'Canal, Holmes? What sort of canal is there in a restaurant?'

'Think of my crossword puzzle clue I was just asking you about. Alimentary, dear Watson.'

Cartoon Corner

What is a 'revoke', Mummy?

ALL MY FAULT

BY P.F. SAUNDERS

I always do my best to win against my granddaughter and young Bruce in our family rubber-bridge four, especially when I am trying to make a contract — but there was one occasion last night when I was delighted to be put down. At first I was both surprised and a little piqued, but I was soon made to change my mind.

I was South, declarer in 4♠; West's opening lead was the ♡8:

♠ A 6 3 2
♡ 10 5 2
◇ A Q 8 3
♣ A K

```
      N
  W       E
      S
```

♠ Q J 10 8 5	**South**	**West**	**North**	**East**
♡ 7 6 4	NB	NB	1◇	1♡
◇ K 4	1♠	NB	3♠	NB
♣ J 9 3	4♠	End		

My first thought was that I was about to lose the first three tricks. After that it must be a simple question of which opponent held the ♠K. If West (Bruce) held it, I would make the remaining ten tricks with five trumps, three diamonds, and two clubs. If East (my granddaughter) had the ♠K, I would go one down. On principle, therefore, I assumed that the all-important card was on my left.

East duly cashed the three top hearts, West discarding a small club. 'What was in your mind,' I asked my granddaughter at the end of the hand, 'before you decided what to lead at trick four?'

'You were in my mind. First, there were your cards. Your bidding showed more than a minimum, so I put you with one of the two missing kings (if you had both, we hadn't a hope) and my partner with the other. The ◇K in his hand wouldn't be much use, and I wasn't going to lead a diamond anyhow. At that point, I very nearly decided to lead a safe club, since the fourth heart would give

35

you a discard (a small diamond, perhaps?) and a ruff in dummy. Then it struck me that Bruce's king, if he had one, might just be the king of trumps — and here's where *you* came in again. You are always telling me to be positive and assume the best. So I assumed that Bruce had the ♠K ...'

'Here, just a minute! That's what I was assuming at exactly the same moment! It seemed my only chance.'

'It seemed my only chance. Your favourite "trump promotion" came to mind, so I did go on after all with a fourth heart.'

Dealer: South
Game All

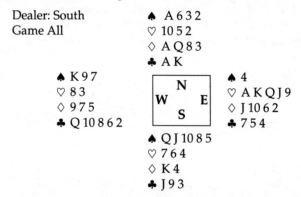

```
                    ♠  A 6 3 2
                    ♡  10 5 2
                    ◇  A Q 8 3
                    ♣  A K
   ♠ K 9 7                          ♠ 4
   ♡ 8 3              N             ♡ A K Q J 9
   ◇ 9 7 5       W        E         ◇ J 10 6 2
   ♣ Q 10 8 6 2        S            ♣ 7 5 4
                    ♠  Q J 10 8 5
                    ♡  7 6 4
                    ◇  K 4
                    ♣  J 9 3
```

I had ruffed the heart lead with the ♠Q, and Bruce had discarded another club. I had then led the ♠J, and this time Bruce had covered, drawing dummy's ace. Nothing could now stop him from defeating the contract with his ♠9.

'So you see,' went on my granddaughter, '*you* are the one responsible for what happened.'

'Not really. What about that partner of yours?' I turned to the silent Bruce. 'Many defenders,' I told him, 'would have eagerly covered my ♠Q when I ruffed the fourth heart. Why didn't you?'

'Don't overruff unless you're sure that it will get you a trick, not lose one.'

'Whom did you get that from, and when?'

'You. Last week.'

For some reason, my granddaughter found this highly amusing, and serious discussion was at an end. The whole thing had made her day ... and mine.

MIKE'S FIRST CAMROSE

BY BOB PITTS

'I think we are going to enjoy ourselves today,' said Mike. 'Yes, I hope so,' agreed Gareth. 'I've never been to an international match before.'

It was the Saturday of the Wales-England Camrose match, the first one to be held in North Wales for several years. Mike and Gareth lived in Ruthin, and had decided to drive over to watch some of the play. Mike played a decent game of bridge and had recently reached the rank of Life Master. Gareth had only been playing for a year, but was progressing well under Mike's guidance.

As Gareth drove, Mike thought about how content he was. His wife had gone out for a game of golf, his son had volunteered to tidy the garden, and even the sun was shining. Everything seemed right with the world.

They had no problem finding the hotel where the match would take place, and Mike noted that they had time to grab a pint before play started. As they entered the hotel bar, Dave Jackson, the match manager, rushed over to him: 'Mike, we've got a bit of a crisis, can you help us out? The problem is that four of the six Welsh players have gone down with some form of food poisoning — even the non-playing captain is affected. We've rung the BBL, the EBU, the WBU, and several Welsh selectors, and the general opinion is that the match must go ahead. Now Berwyn Ross was here to do the Vu-Graph commentary, and he's willing to play. You are certainly the next most experienced Welsh player here; will you play?'

Mike was having trouble finding his voice.

'Look, the England captain is happy for us to field a couple of extra players, and Phil Thomas reckons he'll be fine by this evening, so at most you'll only have to play the first thirty boards.'

'OK then,' croaked Mike.

'Good,' said Dave. 'You've got fifteen minutes to sort out a system with Berwyn, then you're in the open room against John Collings.'

Despite his nerves, all went well for the first few hands, then Mike picked up:

♠ A K J 7 4
♡ J 10 2
◇ A Q 3
♣ 7 5

After two passes, Mike opened with 1♠ and Berwyn jumped to 3◇ to show a good suit with spade support. Mike then bid 4◇, showing the ace. The bidding then continued:

South	West	North	East
NB	NB	1♠	NB
3◇	NB	4◇	NB
4♡	NB	4♠	NB
5♣	NB	6♠	End

Mike awaited the dummy nervously, and was relieved to see the following South hand appear on the table:

♠ Q 9 8 5
♡ A 9 4
◇ K J 10 6 5
♣ Q

He had no trouble making his slam. At the other table, South had opened 1◇ and raised North's 1♠ response to 2♠, and North's 4♠ bid had closed the auction.

Mike was pleased to find that they were ahead after the first two stanzas, and quietly urged himself to keep his concentration for the last ten boards. The seventh board proved to be his biggest problem of the set:

Dealer: South
Love All

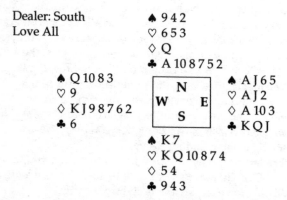

♠ 9 4 2
♡ 6 5 3
◇ Q
♣ A 10 8 7 5 2

♠ Q 10 8 3
♡ 9
◇ K J 9 8 7 6 2
♣ 6

♠ A J 6 5
♡ A J 2
◇ A 10 3
♣ K Q J

♠ K 7
♡ K Q 10 8 7 4
◇ 5 4
♣ 9 4 3

Berwyn had told Mike that the English players would open a Multi 2◇ on very weak hands, often with only a five-card suit. As they had agreed to overcall aggressively against these, Mike felt justified in bidding an immediate 3◇ over South's 2◇ opener. With no way of being sure about a possible grand slam, Berwyn concluded the auction with a jump to 6◇.

North was uncertain about which major suit his partner held, so he started with the ♣A hoping to find a shortage in the opposite hand. The ♣3 from South did nothing to ease North's problem, so he continued with a club, Mike discarding a small spade.

Now, if trumps behaved, it looked like the slam depended solely on the spade finesse, but Mike could see a chance of also making the contract if South held all the major-suit honours. After some thought, he decided that as this was going to be his only Camrose match he would go for it. He played a diamond to his king, a diamond to the ace, and then he cashed the ♠A. He now cashed the third club discarding a spade, and ran the trump suit. South found himself unable to guard both major suits, and the slam was home.

'Well done,' said Berwyn. 'A Vienna Coup. A real journalist's hand. I will put that one in the article I'm writing about the match.'

Wales had won the first match by 17 Victory Points to 13. 'Let me buy you a drink,' said John Collings. 'You deserve it after that set of hands.'

Mike was delighted, people were slapping him on the back, congratulating him and calling his name — Mike! Mike!

'Mike! Wake up, Mike! We're here.' It was Gareth shaking him and trying to wake him up. 'You must have been tired, you've been asleep for the last half-hour. Come on, if we're quick we can grab a pint before the first set of boards.'

Mike dragged himself sleepily into the hotel bar. The match manager came rushing up to him: 'Mike, we've got a bit of a crisis, can you help out?'*

---

*Author's Note: The hands are from the 1996 Wales vs England match which was held at the Risboro Hotel, Llandudno. The event ran without a hitch, the food at the hotel was excellent, and all of the Welsh players selected attended the match.

DISMAL DENNIS IN THE DOG-HOUSE

BY JIMMY ALLAN

When Dismal Dennis failed to appear for coffee we heard about the previous evening's bridge. His partner, the Hospital Superintendent, had been getting more and more irritated by D.D.'s moaning about his poor cards when this hand appeared:

```
Dealer: South          ♠ A K 7 2
N/S Vul.               ♡ 10 4 3
                       ◇ Q 7
                       ♣ K Q 4 2

  ♠ Q J 10                         ♠ 9 6 5 3
  ♡ K J 8 7 5        N             ♡ Q 9 2
  ◇ K 9          W       E         ◇ 6 5 4 2
  ♣ 9 6 5            S             ♣ 8 7

                       ♠ 8 4
                       ♡ A 6
                       ◇ A J 10 8 3
                       ♣ A J 10 3
```

South	West	North	East
1◇	1♡	1♠	NB
2♣	NB	2♡	NB
2NT	NB	3NT	End

Over South's rebid of 2♣, North solved his problem by bidding 2♡ — an enquiry bid. West led the ♠Q and declarer made eleven tricks.

Sitting East, D.D. was disgusted: 'I've averaged just two or three points a hand — my usual luck,' he complained.

The H.S. had kept very quiet, but this was too much for him: 'You are like one of those people who enjoy poor health, but you enjoy poor cards instead,' he said. 'You held the key card to the defence.'

'Me!?' gasped D.D.

'Yes,' replied the H.S. 'Why not double North's 2♡ bid? I would then have led a heart against 3NT.'

Poor D.D. had failed to realise just how helpful a double can be!

HOMAGE TO VICTOR MOLLO

BY ELISABETH AUHAGEN

It was a long rubber-bridge session. The player on my right was dominating the scene holding colossal cards. We already called him Walter the Walrus. Sitting West, I had been dealt one of my usual hands:

♠ Q 4
♡ 10 9 7 4 3
◇ 10 9
♣ Q 9 5 2

The Walrus on my right opened 1NT (16-18) and his sensible partner on my left, who so far had operated without any luck (was his name Karapet?) raised to 3NT and all passed.

I led the ♡4, and dummy came down with:

Dummy
♠ K 7 2
♡ K 5
◇ J 6 4 2
♣ A 8 4 3

The Narrator
♠ Q 4
♡ 10 9 7 4 3
◇ 10 9
♣ Q 9 5 2

```
      N
  W       E
      S
```

Demoralised by dummy's 11 points, I suddenly felt very tired and hungry. I looked for the waiter and ordered almond biscuits. The Walrus, meanwhile, played low from dummy, taking the trick in hand with the ♡Q. A spade to the king was followed by a finesse to the knave, losing to my ♠Q. I persisted with another heart, noting that Walter played the ♡J under dummy's ♡K. When a small club to the knave followed, my biscuits were served and, with a sigh of relief, I started to eat.

'Would you kindly play a card?' my partner (was it the Hog?) asked in a silky voice.

'Oh, excuse me,' I stammered, taking my ♣Q and then leading another heart.

The Walrus discarded a diamond from dummy and took his ♡A. When he hopefully cashed the ♠A, I chose to discard a heart; having recently read an article entitled 'Lavinthal False-cards', I played the ♡10 to show a good holding in diamonds, not clubs.

Declarer now played the ♣K, looked at East's ♣10 with suspicion, and continued with the ♣7. On my ♣5, he looked at the ceiling hoping for inspiration. Finally, he played the ♣A from dummy, and shook his head in disbelief when my partner discarded a small diamond. In desperation, the Walrus now led a diamond; the Hog contributed the ◇7 and declarer ducked. I took my ◇9 and then cashed the good ♣9. The Hog parted with the ♠10 with an air of nonchalance. Would I hear in the post-mortem that I had squeezed him?

Bewildered, I was not sure which red suit to play. Was my ♡9 high already? The avalanche of biscuits had weakened my memory: unfortunately, I no longer remembered which card I had discarded on declarer's ♠A. Suddenly it dawned on me: hadn't I heard a few days ago about a new *Bols* Tip, 'Trust Your Own Lead'? I was sure that I had led hearts, because this had happened before the biscuits appeared.

My nostrils quivering with excitement, I finally tried the ♡9 watching declarer's reaction anxiously. When he discarded a diamond, I realised that I had made five tricks with the two black queens and the three nines in diamonds, clubs, and hearts. Did the bridge rules provide an extra bonus for tricks made in defence with a full house, I wondered?

Karapet bemoaned his bad luck: 'You must have held a bare minimum, Walter,' he commented.

'Only 20 points this time,' broke in the Hog.

A kibitzer with a long nose and a pince-nez remarked: 'Funny hand, going one off in 3NT on a combined 31-count, with the Rabbit taking five tricks on his 4-count and the Hog none, though he held 5 points.'

The full deal was:

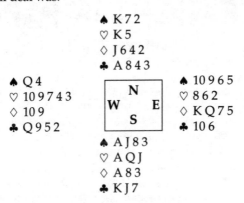

The Hog, of course, had played well at trick ten when he did not split his honours holding the ♠10 and the ◇K-Q. Otherwise declarer can take his ◇A and then exit with a spade, discarding a club from dummy, to score the ◇J at the end.

EAVESDROPPINGS

In an international match against the legendary Italian Blue Team, a French Champion was constantly asking questions about his opponents' bidding. Their replies were always courteous, even when the questions were rather pointless.

After five boards of this, one of the Italian players opened with 1♣, his partner replied 1♠ and the other French player came in with 1NT. Opener doubled, and the French Champion immediately asked: 'What's the meaning of this double?'

'It means,' his opponent told him gravely, 'that we're going to net at least 500!'

'7ST,' *Revista Española de Bridge*

ONE NIGHT IN PARIS

BY SIMON AINGER

Ration Book, petrol coupons, old exam papers, a Christmas card with a solitary X — the sole response of unrequited love. Not really the stuff of history, these relics in the battered suitcase with its broken handle. But, yet. When they come to sort things out, what will they make of the brown envelope containing seven, very dirty, $50 bills and a faded bridge hand?

A television documentary on Harold Macmillan provoked this excursion into the loft. A scandal or two disinterred, but it was the despair of the man when de Gaulle made his historic 'Non' to Britain's application to join the Common Market that pricked the conscience. Three days earlier, they said, everything had been agreed. But had the die been cast more than three months before? And, if conspiracy there was, had I been an unwitting party to it?

Forget the song. Paris in the autumn of 1962 was wet, overpopulated, and thoroughly unwelcoming. The Motor Show was on, the hotels were full, and the only bed available was somewhere towards the end of the *Métro*. I don't remember the name, but *Hotel de la Bastille* would not be inappropriate, although it locked its inmates out rather than in. Both were large, menacing, and inseparable. Donny wouldn't have been seen dead in the place — yet here he was, and obviously as startled to see me as I him.

Before I knew him, Hugh O'Donnell — such was his by-line in print, but he was Donny to all who knew him — had been a distinguished roving correspondent. His obituary in *The Times* would say that he was always first to the telephone. In this he was helped by a daunting physique but, as the years and a love of the good life took their toll, this advantage became a liability. However, a new career was easily available. He called himself an 'international salesman,' though he never revealed what he sold. 'I do deals,' he would reply if anyone asked.

I first met Donny in the bar at the bridge club. He was instantly likeable. With that lilting brogue, retained from a boyhood in Donegal, he could charm a fox from its earth. Since he was at the end of his first career as a journalist and I was at the start of mine with a newsfilm agency, we shared an interest. He played rubber for £1 a hundred, which was way out of my league, but occasionally we were partners at duplicate. He declared 3NT with the same alacrity as he had once commandeered the telephone, but he played the cards well and the blarney excused any disaster.

That day I had returned to the Bastille around 7 o'clock, just as three large men were being let in. The first carried a holdall, the second a suitcase, and the third was ... Donny. He didn't see me at first. The *concierge* and her dog led them straight upstairs, but Donny, at the rear, turned on the first step and our eyes met. He paused, momentarily disconcerted, but then continued. Almost immediately the two heavies came down and left. No one else reappeared, so I went up to my room and lay on the bed and searched for a reason why Donny was here and why he had ignored me. The bedside telephone jangled.

'Come up and have a drink: Room 23.' It was more an order than an invitation but, when I went up a floor, his door was open and he greeted me profusely.

'What in the name of Saint Patrick are you doing here?' he asked.

I explained, and countered with the same question.

'It's convenient,' he replied. 'I've business down the road.'

He produced a bottle of Scotch which we drank neat — 'The water's not to be trusted,' he said — and talked about nothing of consequence. The lousy weather; the *concierge:* 'Céline,' said Donny. 'Reincarnated. *Tricoteuse* in a previous life.' The dog: 'Benito. More bark than bite.' The bottle steadily emptied.

'Right. I'll buy you dinner,' said Donny, suddenly. 'Might even get a game of bridge.'

Already befuddled, I was perhaps surprised that he took the holdall with him and that we set off walking down that forsaken street. We went right and then left and there, flashing its sign, was *The Café de Paris.* Someone's joke. The acrid smell of Gauloises pervaded, even though there were only four men inside. Donny greeted the patron as an old friend and then shook hands with the other three, incongruously dressed in smart suits complete with waistcoats. But we ate, and we drank, on our own; the first — and the last — time I have sampled cous-cous, though the red wine, sandpapering the throat as it went down, anaesthetized the food.

You may understand that the rest of the evening was a blur. I recall going upstairs to play bridge: Donny and I against two of the men. But, after that, I remember only that nothing went right and we lost heavily. Very heavily.

My next recollection was being in bed and wakened by the telephone: 'Sorry to ring so early. We need you back in London. Come back today.'

Dying was the first choice, but this would do. I made it to Orly by mid-afternoon. Donny, I was told when I checked out, had already left.

That night seemed to become unreal, as if it never happened, and I had no contact with Donny. But, three months later, I was on the overnight shift and it was chaotically busy. De Gaulle had dramatically vetoed Britain's application to join the Common Market and miles of newsfilm needed to be processed and cut.

Macmillan was not the only one to have a problem with de Gaulle. He was an editor's nightmare, declaiming, rather than speaking, slowly and at great length. It was a relief when the cutter told me that he had managed to get a short soundbite from his press conference. Fortunately, I checked the edit: 'I have already answered that question.' To be fair, it looked good. Arms aloft, emphatic and theatrical ... 'J'ai déjà repondue ...'

I only looked at mail that had been delivered during the day after making the best of the problems of the night. Nothing of interest ... except for a brown envelope, addressed to me, containing 350 dollars and a hand-written note: 'Your winnings from The Café de Paris. Bien joué. Maigret.'

It must have been another three months before I saw Donny again, once more in the bar of the club. It was to be for the last time. He was as convivial as the first time we had met in the same place, but he was tired and looked ill.

We drank and we talked. About his childhood and his career. About his triumphs and his disasters. About his women and his sins. I listened as his confessor. Eventually and inevitably we had to come to that strange night in Paris. He produced a piece of paper. 'You'll remember this hand,' he said.

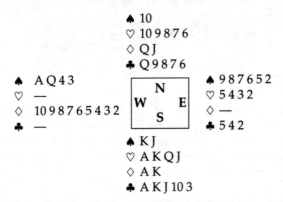

```
            ♠ 10
            ♡ 10 9 8 7 6
            ◊ Q J
            ♣ Q 9 8 7 6
♠ A Q 4 3                    ♠ 9 8 7 6 5 2
♡ —              N           ♡ 5 4 3 2
◊ 10 9 8 7 6 5 4 3 2   W  E  ◊ —
♣ —                 S        ♣ 5 4 2
            ♠ K J
            ♡ A K Q J
            ◊ A K
            ♣ A K J 10 3
```

'I remember eating,' I said, 'but very little about the bridge.'

'Bejasus. Drunk or not, surely nobody forgets a hand with 29 points. You bid 6NT but they sacrificed in 7♠. You doubled, and they made it, of course. A deal of money at a thousand francs a hundred.'

'What!'

'Don't worry. Your losses were paid by a third party. Mine too.'

I looked at the diagram. It was true: there was no defence to the grand slam.

'Naturally, it was fixed,' said Donny.

'Fixed? Third party? Why? What was it all about?'

'That I can't tell you,' he said. 'Maybe one day. And maybe one day we'll be in the Common Market. But not for now. Not in my lifetime.'

'Keep your peace,' he said, and he clasped my shoulder as we parted. At the time I took it as some kind of veiled warning. But perhaps what he said was 'Keep your piece.' If so, I have kept it. Why? Guilt? Because it may be blood money? Then, as now, there were those who wanted us to have nothing to do with Europe. Were they prepared to pay a price to those who might influence the President? What better man than someone who claimed descent from 'Red Hugh' O'Donnell to broker the deal? Losing a fortune at a game of cards.

But, now that I have shared my guilt, it may be time to exorcise it. Accept my *pourboire* graciously — and literally. It should run to a case of champagne.

I HAD A DREAM

BY DAVE HUGGETT

I had a dream last night that I was playing in the final of the World Championships against *very weak* opposition, but mysteriously the outcome of the event depended, I knew with dreadful certainty, upon my ability to bring home the following slam on the very last board:

♠ 3 2
♡ 3 2
◇ 3 2
♣ A J 10 9 8 7 6

♠ A K
♡ A K J 4
◇ A Q J 10 9 8 7
♣ —

My partner had opened 3♣, as they do in these situations, and lacking any scientific approach I had bid 6◇. The ♠J was led and I awaited dummy with trepidation.

The actual sight of the thirteen cards laid out before me was a joy to behold for, barring accidents, I could see that I had a good play for the contract. If hearts broke 4-3, then I could simply ruff a heart in dummy, pitch the losing heart on the ♣A, and take the diamond finesse for a possible overtrick.

However, in such situations it pays to consider what might go wrong, and so I directed my thoughts to the possibility of a 5-2 heart break. Clearly, in that case I would be in danger of losing two trump tricks, but I quickly perceived a possible counter to that situation.

If I played the ◇A before I tried for a heart ruff, then I would still succeed if my left-hand opponent with two hearts had either a singleton trump, or king doubleton, or even no trumps at all, or if my right-hand opponent with two hearts had any singleton or a void in trumps.

Estimating the odds has never been one of my strong points, but as I considered the overall chances of success to be overwhelmingly in my favour, I set out upon my course of action without delay.

The ♡A passed off quietly, but upon the play of the ♡K my right-hand opponent contributed the ♡Q. Had that, I wondered, made a significant difference? I was about to embark upon my original plan and cash the ◇A, when I realised that this extra piece of information had indeed altered the odds.

For now, as I saw with blinding clarity, I had a chance to make my contract if East had an original trump holding of a void, king singleton, king doubleton, or king to three. I would lead the ♡J and discard dummy's second spade: if East did not ruff, I would continue by ruffing my remaining top spade, pitch the ♡4 on the ♣A, and then take the trump finesse. If East ruffed the ♡J and played back a trump, I would successfully finesse, cross to dummy with the spade ruff, discard the ♡4 on the ♣A, and then continue by ruffing a club to hand and drawing trumps. If, finally, East ruffed but did not play back a trump, I would be able to enter dummy with a spade ruff, dispose of my losing heart on the ♣A, and take the diamond finesse.

I decided to go ahead with my revised plan, aware that I was taking the risk of giving East the opportunity of making a small singleton trump. Imagining the respectful hush in the Vu-Graph room, I considered my course of action and held my head in my hands to add verisimilitude to the aura of intense concentration which I was trying to convey, for I knew by now that the closed-circuit television operators would have zoomed in close upon my studied brow.

Finally, with a deep sigh and a theatrical gesture made to indicate that these things come easily to me, I did lead the ♡J intending to discard dummy's remaining spade, only to find that it was *West* who ruffed, while East contributed a small heart with an embarrassed air.

I pitched the spade as intended, and when West returned a spade I ruffed in dummy and discarded my losing heart on the ♣A — and now, with a dreadful sense of foreboding, I led a diamond to my queen and West's king. I was one down!

My right-hand opponent was peering through the hole in the screen that divides the table and whispering to his partner: 'I'm so sorry about my play,' he said. 'I had the hearts and the diamonds all muddled up, and I thought I only had two hearts. Still, I don't think it mattered as it happens. Do you think we won?'

I later found out that the complete hand was:

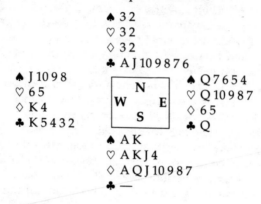

```
                    ♠ 3 2
                    ♡ 3 2
                    ◇ 3 2
                    ♣ A J 10 9 8 7 6
    ♠ J 10 9 8              ♠ Q 7 6 5 4
    ♡ 6 5         N         ♡ Q 10 9 8 7
    ◇ K 4      W     E      ◇ 6 5
    ♣ K 5 4 3 2    S        ♣ Q
                    ♠ A K
                    ♡ A K J 4
                    ◇ A Q J 10 9 8 7
                    ♣ —
```

PRACTICE MAKES PERFECT

In a teams match one pair managed to play Boards 1-7 out of eight, and then lift Board 1 onto the table again instead of Board 8.

Well, we've all done that, haven't we. Some of us, like this pair, have probably even re-played the board. However, first time around the intrepid heroes of this story gained 300 on the board but in the replay, with the benefit of hindsight, they converted this into minus 200.

Fortunately they were not required to play the board again, when a really bad score might have been achieved.

The Bradford Kibbitzer

THE PELICAN CUP

BY AUDREY AND MARTIN HOFFMAN

The finals of the Pelican Bridge Club end-of-season championship saw the clash of two strong teams in a memorable match. The *Floridian Team* was captained, as usual, by Able Mabel. She lives up to her name, being an excellent organiser and fine card player who always manages to field a top team. Although the Floridians nearly always have only four players, they do very well and all have the stamina of teenagers, although none of them is under 55.

Mabel's partner, rather unfairly named Dopey Dora (except for her looks) is very dynamic at the table. Her judgement is astounding, and she throws the opponents into many a quandary. She always — no matter how well you know her — seems to use her looks to tremendous advantage: half the time she looks as though she is in another world, but woe betide the unwary opponents.

Richard the Lionheart is a slow and deliberate player who often, unlike his Captain, takes ages to play the hand. Fortunately he plays mostly in teams games where slow play is less of a problem than at pairs.

His partner Gott in Himmel, like his nickname, is always courteous to the opponents. He tends to put them so much at ease that they underestimate his often superior talent. He excels in defence, and claims that this is because in his rubber-bridge days he never got good cards.

The *Northern Snowbirds* come down to sunny Florida for several months in the winter to indulge in their favourite hobbies — golf, tennis, and last but not least bridge. The players are a mixed bunch, and never get together outside Florida. Usually the team comprises Captain Buffalo Bill and his French-Canadian partner Montreal Monty, together with Toronto Tammy and Mississauga Minny. Occasionally, they are joined by Winnipeg Wyn and Raging Reg from Niagara Falls.

The match was played at the Pelican Bridge Club and the two deals below were the crucial ones in deciding the winners of the event:

Dopey Dora
♠ 3 2
♡ K Q 3 2
◇ A K 10 4
♣ 7 5 2

```
      N
  W       E
      S
```

Able Mabel

♠ A	South	West	North	East
♡ A 4	1◇	NB	1♡	NB
◇ 9 8 7 6 5	2♣	NB	3◇	NB
♣ A Q 9 8 6	4♣	NB	5◇	End

West led the ♠Q. Mabel won and played a trump to West's ◇Q, dummy's ◇K, and East's ◇2. She now ruffed a spade, and then played the ♡A, a heart to the ♡Q, and a small heart which she ruffed in hand. Dummy was re-entered with the ace of trumps, on which West discarded a spade. Next the ♡K was led; East did not ruff, and Mabel just discarded a club and then played the ♣2 to her ♣8.

West won with the ♣J, but he was endplayed: a spade lead would give declarer a ruff and discard, and a club exit would give her two club tricks for the contract.

The full deal was:

Dealer: South
Game All

Dopey Dora
♠ 3 2
♡ K Q 3 2
◇ A K 10 4
♣ 7 5 2

Toronto Tammy
♠ Q J 10 9 8
♡ J 9 7 5
◇ Q
♣ K J 3

```
      N
  W       E
      S
```

Mississauga Minny
♠ K 7 6 5 4
♡ 10 8 6
◇ J 3 2
♣ 10 4

Able Mabel
♠ A
♡ A 4
◇ 9 8 7 6 5
♣ A Q 9 8 6

In the replay, the same contract was reached. Sitting West was Richard the Lionheart. He took some time before making the opening lead, but finally emerged with the queen of trumps — a devastating move, as it removed a vital entry prematurely. Declarer could not develop the ending reached by Mabel and the contract failed for a big swing.

This was the other hand which decided the outcome:

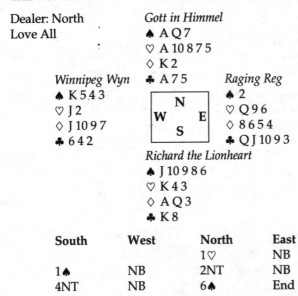

Dealer: North
Love All

Gott in Himmel
♠ A Q 7
♡ A 10 8 7 5
◇ K 2
♣ A 7 5

Winnipeg Wyn
♠ K 5 4 3
♡ J 2
◇ J 10 9 7
♣ 6 4 2

Raging Reg
♠ 2
♡ Q 9 6
◇ 8 6 5 4
♣ Q J 10 9 3

Richard the Lionheart
♠ J 10 9 8 6
♡ K 4 3
◇ A Q 3
♣ K 8

South	West	North	East
		1♡	NB
1♠	NB	2NT	NB
4NT	NB	6♠	End

West led the ◇J. Richard won in hand with the queen and ran the ♠J followed by another spade. When East failed to follow, the contract appeared to be doomed. The only chance seemed to be finding the ♡Q-J doubleton in either hand, or a singleton heart honour with East. This was unlikely, as East had already shown up with a singleton spade. As usual, Richard took his time, but eventually he saw a glimmer of hope.

He cashed the ◇K, then led a club to the ♣K, ♣8 to ♣A, and ruffed a club. He then cashed the ◇A, throwing a heart from dummy. Next came ♡K and a heart to the ace, followed by a heart exit. East was now on lead in this two-card ending:

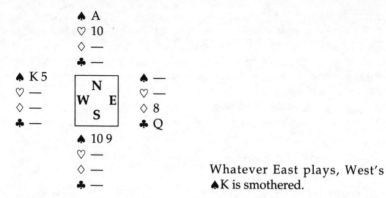

```
              ♠ A
              ♡ 10
              ◇ —
              ♣ —
♠ K 5         ┌─────────┐      ♠ —
♡ —           │    N    │      ♡ —
◇ —           │ W     E │      ◇ 8
♣ —           │    S    │      ♣ Q
              └─────────┘
              ♠ 10 9
              ♡ —
              ◇ —
              ♣ —
```

Whatever East plays, West's ♠K is smothered.

As the opponents in the other room stopped in game, the resulting swing was sufficient to give Able Mabel's team victory in a very tough match.

Cartoon Corner

Am I too late for the Bermuda Bowl?

SLEEPING PARTNERS

BY MALCOLM SIMPSON

'I'm amazed at you!' remarked Dr Crowe, staring in my direction.' 'You have more points than either of our good ladies, yet you fail to make a bid — 5◇ is cold. Not only that, you make the one lead to make my contract a virtual lay-down, as the cards lie!'

Dealer: East
Love All

Mrs Crowe
♠ 7 6 4
♡ A Q 6 4
◇ 7 6
♣ K 10 7 2

The Author
♠ 5 2
♡ K J 8 5 3
◇ A 2
♣ A 9 8 6

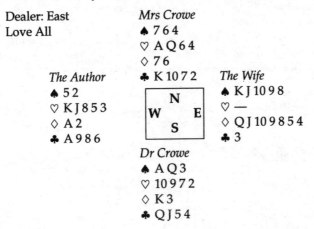

The Wife
♠ K J 10 9 8
♡ —
◇ Q J 10 9 8 5 4
♣ 3

Dr Crowe
♠ A Q 3
♡ 10 9 7 2
◇ K 3
♣ Q J 5 4

I have frequently lectured the Wife about not pre-empting in a minor when holding a four-card major. As the East hand does not fall into that category, she opened 3◇. My boss, not uncharacteristically, bid 3NT. Mrs Crowe passed less comfortably than myself, and the Wife, disregarding further lectures about not bidding twice with a pre-emptive hand, doubled.

Being promised a seven-card suit, I opened the defence with ace and another diamond. Dr Crowe won trick two with the ◇K and conceded a trick to my ♣A. I led a spade, but there was no entry to my partner's hand and Dr Crowe made nine tricks via the spade finesse, two heart finesses, three clubs, and that wretched ◇K.

'An obvious simple passive lead and my double would probably have been successful!' growled the Wife.

'I reckon you'll be kicked out into the spare bedroom tonight!' grinned Dr Crowe.

GIVE THE OPPOSITION A CHANCE

BY LEN ARMSTRONG

'Well, we can't win them all,' said Stephy Redwood. 'Eight IMPs down and this last one must be flat.'

Her husband, David, smiled and said, 'Well?'

'Board 16, +100 to us,' continued Stephy.

'And +620; that's 720, which is twelve IMPs. We win by four IMPs.'

Following this conversation, Wilma Baumgarten spread the hands from Board 16 upon the table as follows:

Dealer: South
Game All

Mike
(Pat Marksom)
- ♠ K Q 5 3
- ♡ K 4
- ◇ A 9 4
- ♣ K J 5 3

Ginny Leese
(Stephy)
- ♠ 8 4
- ♡ 8 3 2
- ◇ K J 8
- ♣ 10 9 8 7 2

Mal Leese
(Wilma)
- ♠ 7
- ♡ A J 10 7 6 5
- ◇ Q 5 3
- ♣ A 6 4

```
      N
  W       E
      S
```

David
(Morris Marksom)
- ♠ A J 10 9 6 2
- ♡ Q 9
- ◇ 10 7 6 2
- ♣ Q

The bidding had been identical at both tables:

South	West	North	East
NB	NB	1♣	1♡
1♠	NB	3♠	NB
4♠	End		

'Stephy,' said Wilma, 'had to avoid misleading me. She chose to lead the ♡8 despite the danger that she would have to peter if two

56

rounds of hearts were played. This would falsely suggest she had led from a doubleton and could ruff a third heart. Had she made a MUD lead of the ♡3, I might have thought that she held an honour in hearts. Morris Marksom, the declarer, played the ♡K from dummy. I took with the ace, switched to a diamond, and he now had to lose two diamonds and the ♣A to go one down. We assumed it would be flat.'

'Declarer at your table never enlisted your help,' said David. 'He gave you no chance to go wrong.'

'Come on then, smarty-pants,' said his wife. 'How did *you* make the contract?'

'I also got the lead of the ♡8 but I played low from dummy, leaving Mal Leese with a problem. If his partner had led the ♡8 from a doubleton, then putting up his ♡A would establish my king and queen. He chose, as many defenders would, to play the ♡10, reserving his ace for dummy's king.'

'End of the tale, then,' said Wilma. 'You won in hand with the ♡Q, drew trumps, and led the ♣Q. Ten tricks made.'

'Spot on!' said David. 'Now what about Board 14, where you went two ...'

EAVESDROPPINGS

'You play the cards so well, partner,' said West ingratiatingly as he put down a very poor dummy. Flattered, East smiled: 'Oh yes,' she said. 'I've heard this remark before.'

'But not, I believe,' murmured North, 'addressed to you!'

Chris Kinloch

IT HAPPENED ONE NIGHT

*D*id you find some of the plays and situations
described in 'Bridge Fiction' hard to believe? Well,
*you haven't seen anything yet! They say that 'truth is
stranger than fiction', and this is certainly true in bridge
— as the following real-life stories will show.*

IT HAPPENED THAT WAY

BY FREDDIE NORTH

Throughout the years, generation after generation, bridge has produced many charismatic characters who do much to enrich the general scene. Scattered amongst these star players are a few genuine eccentrics who also make a lively contribution to the fund of incredible stories that go the rounds. Perhaps the most remarkable example of eccentricity occurred in London some years ago, when our hero occupied the West seat in the following hand:

Rubber Bridge
Dealer: South
N/S Vul.

♠ K J 10 9 6 4
♡ K J 9 5 3
♢ 6
♣ 4

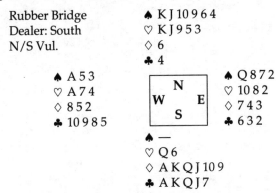

♠ A 5 3
♡ A 7 4
♢ 8 5 2
♣ 10 9 8 5

♠ Q 8 7 2
♡ 10 8 2
♢ 7 4 3
♣ 6 3 2

♠ —
♡ Q 6
♢ A K Q J 10 9
♣ A K Q J 7

The bidding can only be described as a chapter of accidents. South opened 2♣, North responded 2♠, and then it continued 3♢ — 3♡ — 4♣ — 4♡. At this point South decided it was time for a Blackwood 4NT, but with no suit agreed North took this as a natural bid and continued with 5♡. 'Knowing' the partnership held all the aces, South wasted no more time and bid 7NT, and West was equally quick to double. So far nothing terribly eccentric had happened; there had just been a monumental muddle in the auction.

Eccentric or not, West certainly knew a good thing when he saw it and was anxious to savour the moment. It seemed that there was no great rush to cash his aces — anyone could do that — so he led the ♣10!

As the dummy went down declarer somehow managed to maintain a poker face. The ♣A took the first trick and the spotlight returned to our eccentric hero when the ♡6 appeared on the table at trick two. Perhaps feeling that his partner might hold the ♡Q, but in any case seeing no urgency to rush in with his ace, West played low and dummy won with the king. For a moment or two time stood still, and then the avalanche of minor-suit winners followed one after the other, so that at trick twelve this was the position, with West still clutching his two aces:

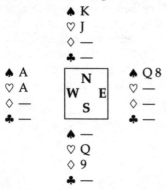

As declarer produced the ◊9 the awful truth dawned on West. He wasn't going to make both his aces after all. Worse still, he didn't know which one to throw!

Once again time stood still as West agonised on which ace to jettison. First one card was fingered, then the other. The ceiling was consulted, as players will when searching for inspiration, but obviously there was no help forthcoming from that quarter. Eventually — yes, you've guessed it — our hero discarded the ♡A and retained the ♠A.

Oh dear! You should have seen East's face!

IF ONLY

BY WARNER SOLOMON

Playing with my wife Louise in the Life Masters Pairs in Coventry, with three rounds to go and in close contention I held the South hand below:

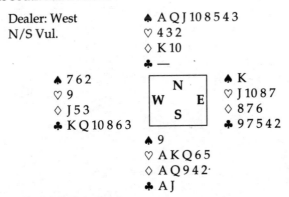

Dealer: West
N/S Vul.

North:
♠ A Q J 10 8 5 4 3
♡ 4 3 2
♢ K 10
♣ —

West:
♠ 7 6 2
♡ 9
♢ J 5 3
♣ K Q 10 8 6 3

East:
♠ K
♡ J 10 8 7
♢ 8 7 6
♣ 9 7 5 4 2

South:
♠ 9
♡ A K Q 6 5
♢ A Q 9 4 2·
♣ A J

The bidding proceeded:

South	West	North	East
	3♣	4♠	5♣
6♠	NB	NB	7♣
NB*	NB	7♠	NB
7NT	End		

*Forcing

The ♣K is led. Five rounds of diamonds and three rounds of hearts are played and, if the ♣2 which East played at trick one can be trusted as a true card, then West's distribution is known to be 3-1-3-6. The only chance to make the contract, therefore, is to drop the ♠K singleton. This is how Garozzo would have played it.

I finessed the spade at trick two and went six down.

A double of 7♣ would have yielded 1700. Two chances to win!

GOOD LEAD, PARTNER!

BY DAVID PERKINS

The importance of making the right opening lead was dramatically demonstrated on the following hand from a local pairs event:

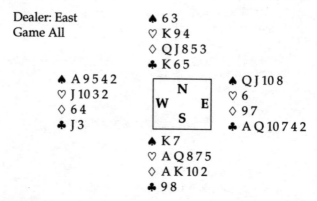

Dealer: East
Game All

```
            ♠ 6 3
            ♡ K 9 4
            ◇ Q J 8 5 3
            ♣ K 6 5

♠ A 9 5 4 2              ♠ Q J 10 8
♡ J 10 3 2              ♡ 6
◇ 6 4         N         ◇ 9 7
♣ J 3      W   E       ♣ A Q 10 7 4 2
              S
            ♠ K 7
            ♡ A Q 8 7 5
            ◇ A K 10 2
            ♣ 9 8
```

The bidding went:

South	West	North	East
			NB
1♡	NB	2◇	Dbl
3◇	3♠	NB	NB
3NT	Dbl	End	

West made a 'sporting' double when South essayed 3NT. Equally sportingly, South stood it.

Since South was obviously prepared for a spade lead, West led the ♣J. After taking his six club tricks, East had little difficulty in switching to the ♠Q. South clung stubbornly to his two red aces, and made them both at tricks twelve and thirteen.

Plus 2000 was a top for East-West, disappointing those pairs who played and made 4♠ — doubled or not. Some North-Souths scored plus 600 in 3NT when West led a spade.

Since West was notoriously slow to praise partner, East remained silent — but West knew what he must be thinking!

GAMESWOMANSHIP

BY KITTY TELTSCHER

The *Barnardo's Evening of Bridge*, staged in January 1996, was a glittering event which attracted top bridge players including Zia Mahmood, Robert Sheehan, Bob Hamman, Tony Priday, Nicola Smith, Michele Handley, and many other stars as well as a host of less illustrious, but enthusiastic players. Altogether two hundred and forty people were playing in the duplicate.

It was a rare treat to see so many bridge players elegantly clad, sipping champagne, in the imposing and extraordinarily beautiful surroundings of Draper's Hall.

The format was a 16-board Chicago Duplicate, and the winners were Robert Sheehan playing with Martin Barber and Tony Priday playing with Arthur Goddard.

Arthur had a very interesting hand early in the evening, when, sitting South, dealer, he picked up:

	South	West	North	East
♠ A J 3	2♣	2◇	NB	NB
♡ A K Q 9 7 4	2♡	NB	4♡	NB
◇ 9	4NT	NB	5◇	NB
♣ A K Q	6♡	End		

West led the ◇K, and this is what declarer saw:

♠ 10 8 7 4
♡ J 6 3
◇ A 4
♣ J 10 9 8

```
    N
W       E
    S
```

♠ A J 3
♡ A K Q 9 7 4
◇ 9
♣ A K Q

Goddard won the trick with the ◇A, then played a small diamond on which he discarded the ♣A! After that the contract was unbeatable.

Declarer won the spade return in hand, cashed the ♡A-K, ♣K-Q, and crossed to dummy with the ♡J. Then he cashed the ♣J-10, discarding his two spade losers. By discarding the ♣A, he had unblocked the suit.

The full deal was:

Dealer: South
N/S Vul.

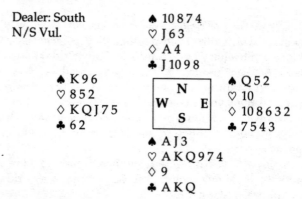

```
                    ♠ 10 8 7 4
                    ♡ J 6 3
                    ◇ A 4
                    ♣ J 10 9 8
♠ K 9 6                              ♠ Q 5 2
♡ 8 5 2          N                   ♡ 10
◇ K Q J 7 5   W     E                ◇ 10 8 6 3 2
♣ 6 2            S                   ♣ 7 5 4 3
                    ♠ A J 3
                    ♡ A K Q 9 7 4
                    ◇ 9
                    ♣ A K Q
```

At many other tables, a less successful line was taken: the diamond lead was won, the ♡A-K cashed, and then the ♣A-K-Q were played. This line depends on either trumps breaking, or clubs breaking, or the long clubs being held by the defender with the last trump. The problem is that the diamond lead takes one entry out of dummy and the club suit is effectively blocked.

Also playing was Vivian Priday, partnered by Richard Coe. Vivian, Tony Priday's vivacious and glamorous wife, is a naturally gifted player who displays tremendous panache and style, especially in her bidding.

On the same hand, Vivian and Richard reached 7♣, which Vivian made for a complete top. 'How did you reach 7♣?' asked her husband.

'Easily,' Vivian said sweetly. 'I'm rather surprised *you* missed it!'

THE LUCK OF THE CARDS

BY PETER DONOVAN

Utopia came to Lords' last year, when MCC opened the doors of the home of cricket to bridge. My two great loves now under one roof — and an added opportunity for ladies to visit our 'hallowed' Pavilion!

Bridge is never boring or dull in the Club, and a recent match in our current rubber bridge competition demonstrated that the game can be just as exciting as a NatWest Final.

Let me set the scene for you. Your match lasts for six rubbers or three hours, whichever is the shorter. After five rubbers, you are 1210 points adrift with forty minutes remaining on the clock. By the time you call 'Last two hands,' you are Game All in the last rubber — but still 930 behind — so the match to all intents and purposes is lost, for only a slam will do. Then LHO deals you this hand:

♠ 6
♡ K Q 4
◇ A K Q J 7 6 3
♣ K 5

While you are working out what devious action you can take to save the day, your partner opens 1NT (weak)! What would you have bid?

You might reasonably feel that a direct raise to 6◇ was called for — because there could never be another chance like this. However, the devious cricket mind of our would-be declarer reasoned that it was just possible that partner held no aces; if this was the case, he didn't even want to be in game — there was still one more deal remaining. So he bid a Gerber 4♣, not certain whether partner remembered the convention. He would pass 4◇, and keep his fingers crossed with 6◇ after a 4♡ bid. He needn't have worried. This was partner's hand:

♠ A K 4
♡ A J 8 3
◇ 9 8
♣ Q 8 6 2

MCC bridge is always played in humorous mode, as shown by the following bit of supper repartee.

North to West: 'Sorry, I've been using your side plate.' West: 'Don't worry, I've been eating your sandwiches.' (It never sounds so funny in print!)

TIME TO THINK

BY EDWARD HORSUP

L ike driving a car, speed at the bridge table is an individual matter. People tolerate slow play, or get exasperated, for different reasons.

A charming lady at a well-known club where I often play is never guilty of taking a decision without careful thought. When I found her Director for the evening, hopes of an early night were at once abandoned. Yet the majesty of office worked wonders: not only did the lady play a good deal faster than her norm; she kept the movement going with a courteous briskness that was an example to all Directors. She even found time to work out a fine defence when I was at her table:

```
Dealer: North          ♠ Q 7 5
Game All               ♡ 8 3 2
                       ◇ A K Q J 9 8
                       ♣ A

   ♠ J 10 8 3                        ♠ K 6 2
   ♡ J 10 9 6 4      N               ♡ A Q 5
   ◇ 10 5        W       E           ◇ 7 4
   ♣ 7 6            S                ♣ J 8 5 3 2

                       ♠ A 9 4
                       ♡ K 7
                       ◇ 6 3 2
                       ♣ K Q 10 9 4
```

South	West	North	East
		1◇	NB
2♣	NB	3◇	NB
4NT	NB	5♡	NB
6NT	End		

In an uncontested auction, partner opened 1◇ and I responded 2♣. Hoping for glittering diamonds after partner's jump rebid, I launched us into a slam. When West led the ♡J, you can work out the likely result. East would take the ♡A and return a heart. A stream of diamonds would then squeeze her into giving up a club trick or else baring the ♠K.

Not our doughty Director. After a not-unreasonable time to think, she ducked the heart lead. With no option, I took my king and reeled off the diamonds.

East discarded both the ♡A and ♡Q after the spade and club that could be spared. This was the six-card ending, with the lead in dummy:

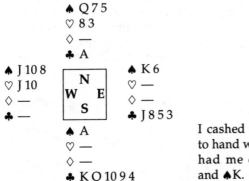

```
              ♠ Q 7 5
              ♡ 8 3
              ◇ —
              ♣ A
♠ J 10 8                   ♠ K 6
♡ J 10      ┌─────────┐    ♡ —
◇ —         │    N    │    ◇ —
♣ —         │  W   E  │    ♣ J 8 5 3
            │    S    │
            └─────────┘
              ♠ A
              ♡ —
              ◇ —
              ♣ K Q 10 9 4
```

I cashed the ♣A and got back to hand with the ♠A. The finale had me conceding to the ♣J and ♠K.

Yes — had I discarded the ♣4 to keep ♠A-x, I could have made the contract with a spade throw-in, but greedy for thirteen tricks, I elected to bare the ♠A.

If this had been a major event instead of an ordinary club duplicate, East would have been running strongly for a brilliancy prize. It was a privilege to have been defeated thus. No-one else was in the slam: the par score was 3NT plus three.

MEMORABLE QUOTES

'According to an evening paper, there are only five real authorities on bridge in this country. Odd how often one gets one of them as partner!'

Punch (quoted in *Points Schmoints!*
Bergen's Winning Bridge Secrets by Marty Bergen)

MY 'UNFORGETTABLE' CONVENTION

BY AMANDA HAWTHORN

Modern tournament players have available to them a bewildering choice of conventions and there is much scope for misunderstanding. There are some conventions, though, which are so plainly not natural bids that confusion should not arise. Or so I thought when I picked up the South hand below at my local club:

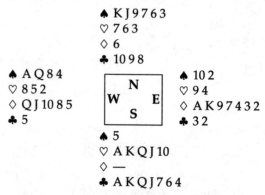

```
                    ♠ K J 9 7 6 3
                    ♡ 7 6 3
                    ◇ 6
                    ♣ 10 9 8
     ♠ A Q 8 4            N           ♠ 10 2
     ♡ 8 5 2        W         E       ♡ 9 4
     ◇ Q J 10 8 5        S           ◇ A K 9 7 4 3 2
     ♣ 5                              ♣ 3 2
                    ♠ 5
                    ♡ A K Q J 10
                    ◇ —
                    ♣ A K Q J 7 6 4
```

As I was contemplating my cards, RHO, as dealer, opened with 3◇. I have a textbook hand for an overcall of 4NT which, like the opening bid of 4NT, shows eleven or twelve certain tricks and demands that partner cue-bid an ace if he holds one.

My partner failed to alert my bid and LHO bid 6◇, over which partner briskly volunteered 6♠. I hopefully bid 7♣ and all passed. The ◇Q was led, dummy went down minus the ♠A — and so, therefore, did the contract!

There were many different results on the traveller: 6♡ was our par spot, but the popular contract was 7♣ minus one, both doubled and undoubled. No-one played in 7◇ doubled which, I was assured by our opponents, would have been the contract at our table had I been able to bid 6♡. You see, my opponents knew my 'unforgettable' convention — alas that one of them was not my partner on that night!

70

THE VICTIMS
BY TONY PRIDAY

The unluckiest pair at the 15th Marbella Festival of Bridge was Alvaro Fresneda, and his partner Luca de Tena. Leading the field in the Open Pairs, they met Peter Matthews and myself in the final round, only to become victims of my forgetfulness as South:

```
Dealer: West          ♠ K J 10 5 2
N/S Vul.              ♡ A 9 7 6
                     ◊ 9
                     ♣ 10 8 4

♠ 9 4 3          N           ♠ 8 7
♡ Q 8 3 2    W       E       ♡ K 10 5
◊ 10 8 4         S           ◊ A Q 7 3
♣ 7 6 5                      ♣ K Q 3 2

                     ♠ A Q 6
                     ♡ J 4
                     ◊ K J 6 5 2
                     ♣ A J 9
```

South	West	North	East
	NB	NB	1◊
1NT	NB	2♣	NB
2◊	NB	3♡	NB
3NT	End		

At the end of the bidding my American partner announced alarmingly: 'There has been a failure to alert!' I had forgotten we were playing the Smolen convention whereby Stayman is followed by a jump in the shorter major of 5-4. Obviously I should have bid 4♠; as it was, I needed to make ten tricks in no-trumps.

West led the ◊4 and East won the ◊A, and switched to the ♣K. I won the ♣A and ran my spades. At trick eight I led a club from dummy and East took the ♣Q and exited with his last club. After winning the ♣J, I led a heart to the ♡A. To avoid being endplayed East unblocked the ♡K but I then led a heart to the ♡10, ♡J, and ♡Q. Miraculously, dummy's ♡9-7 now sat over West's ♡8-3 and took the last two tricks!

IT HAPPENED ONE MONDAY NIGHT

BY PETER LITTLEWOOD

Sheffield is one of the fortresses of Yorkshire bridge, with strength in depth, which is illustrated by the success of the Sheffield and District League for teams of four. It has six divisions. The first division produces a real battle every season, with one Monday evening set aside each month for the various encounters.

In the first match of the season, sitting South on the following board, you eventually become declarer in an aggressive and rather precarious 4♠, the opposition having been silent throughout. You should cover up the East-West cards if you want to test your dummy play.

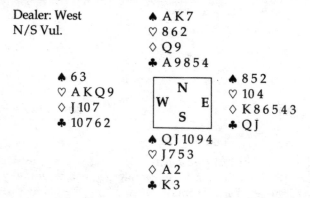

```
Dealer: West        ♠ A K 7
N/S Vul.            ♡ 8 6 2
                    ◇ Q 9
                    ♣ A 9 8 5 4

♠ 6 3                            ♠ 8 5 2
♡ A K Q 9          N             ♡ 10 4
◇ J 10 7       W       E         ◇ K 8 6 5 4 3
♣ 10 7 6 2         S             ♣ Q J

                    ♠ Q J 10 9 4
                    ♡ J 7 5 3
                    ◇ A 2
                    ♣ K 3
```

Against your 4♠, West leads ♡A-K-Q-9, forcing you to ruff high in dummy. East has discarded two low diamonds, so what is your plan of campaign?

That was the start at both tables, stopping the Souths from even thinking about setting up the club suit, and leaving a squeeze against West the only possibility left open for each declarer. With East being able to discard after dummy, and consequently under no stress, West would have to be the target of any squeeze. Therefore, the trumps were run to leave this position before the last one was played:

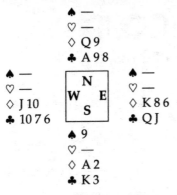

```
              ♠ —
              ♡ —
              ◇ Q 9
              ♣ A 9 8
♠ —                        ♠ —
♡ —          N            ♡ —
◇ J 10    W     E         ◇ K 8 6
♣ 10 7 6     S            ♣ Q J
              ♠ 9
              ♡ —
              ◇ A 2
              ♣ K 3
```

At the first table in the above position, South wrongly made the Vienna Coup play of the ◇A, so, not holding the ◇K, West was not under any pressure when the last trump was played.

At the second table, the last trump was played off and the ◇10 appeared from West. South had already decided that West could not, or should not, hold the ◇K — otherwise, with 12 points, he would have opened the bidding at favourable vulnerability.

As a consequence, declarer discarded a club from dummy, then entered dummy via the ♣A to lead the ◇Q, pinning West's ◇J for the contract.

Regardless of the type of play involved, which may look complex, the key to success was the simple counting of West's hand.

An important aspect of declarer play is counting the opposition's high-card points, but it is an area which many players overlook at the table.

EAVESDROPPINGS

When it became clear that North was too busy with her own thoughts to realise that she was the dealer, her partner leaned across the table: 'Your go!' he said.

Promptly, North led the ♠A.

Mike Swanson

RUFF RECORD

BY ALAN A. BROWN

It was the qualifying round for a County event at our club, and I heard my RHO, as dealer, open a weak 3♣. My South hand was:

♠ —
♡ A K 8 7 6 2
◇ K 10 5 4
♣ K 10 7

Now I have played with this gentleman, and I know that he plays it by the book — his pre-empts are weak and normally based on a seven-card suit.

We usually play Fishbein for take-out, but I was pretty certain that partner would reply spades, so I just bid a simple 4♡. LHO now bid 5♣, and partner, with minimal pause for thought, jumped to 6♡. This went round to LHO who doubled and led the ♠A.

♠ 10 8 7 6 4 3
♡ Q 10 9 3
◇ 3
♣ A 2

```
        N
   W         E
        S
```

♠ —
♡ A K 8 7 6 2
◇ K 10 5 4
♣ K 10 7

South	West	North	East
			3♣
4♡	5♣	6♡	NB
NB	Dbl	End	

Looking at dummy, I apply Rule No. 1: Count Your Tricks. I have eight on top, and I need four more. Diamond ruffs in dummy — that's three. A club ruff in dummy? No, that's out, because West can have one club at most. Can I set the spades up? Well, nobody has bid them. Surely if West had five or six he would have bid them over 4♡, so he probably only has three or four. And he must have the ◇A for his double. Similarly, East is known to have seven clubs. Give him the remaining three or four spades, and I can imagine a shortage of hearts there.

Anyway, I need four ruffs to set up the spades; have I got

enough entries? Hopefully, trumps themselves will provide them, plus the ♣A which ought to stand up.

I start by ruffing the first spade in hand and immediately lead a small club. West plays the ♣J, and I win in dummy and lead another spade for a second ruff, both opponents following. Having removed West's club, I cannot afford to let East in to lead one, so I play the ◇K which is taken by West. He now leads a heart, won by dummy's ♡9 with East showing out. I can see my way clear now, so I ruff another spade with the ♡A, both opponents following, back to dummy with a diamond ruff, ruff out the last spade with my ♡K, lead a small heart to dummy finessing the ♡10, draw the last trump and claim. The full deal was:

Dealer: East   ♠ 10 8 7 6 4 3
N/S Vul.   ♡ Q 10 9 3
               ◇ 3
               ♣ A 2

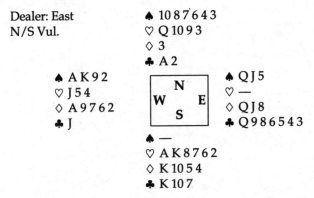

♠ A K 9 2   ♠ Q J 5
♡ J 5 4   ♡ —
◇ A 9 7 6 2   ◇ Q J 8
♣ J   ♣ Q 9 8 6 5 4 3

               ♠ —
               ♡ A K 8 7 6 2
               ◇ K 10 5 4
               ♣ K 10 7

I have made dummy reversals before, but not with quite as many ruffs as that. And 6♡ doubled and made on a combined 19 count can't be all that bad either, can it?

GOOD TIMING ... NOT

BY MARC SMITH

D r Akram Zaman originally hails from India, and therefore does not have the usual Gaelic traits of fair skin and red hair, but having lived in Cardiff for many years he considers himself Welsh.

His superb timing of the play on this hand from a recent trip to Ostend, Belgium, for the European Union Championships, illustrates why his team-mates are happy to acknowledge him as at least an Honorary Welshman:

Dealer: West
Game All

Mike Hirst
♠ J 10 9 2
♡ J 5 3
◇ K 7 4
♣ A 6 2

♠ A K 8 5 4
♡ 9 8 6 2
◇ Q 3 2
♣ 8

```
        N
    W       E
        S
```

♠ Q 7 3
♡ K 10 7 4
◇ 10 6
♣ Q J 10 7

Akram Zaman
♠ 6
♡ A Q
◇ A J 9 8 5
♣ K 9 5 4 3

South	West	North	East
	NB	NB	NB
1◇	1♠	1NT	NB
2♣	NB	3◇	NB
5◇	End		

Even looking at all four hands, it is not easy to see how declarer can make eleven tricks, but Zaman demonstrated how it could be done — and without any help from East-West!

West led the ♠K and switched to a heart, declarer winning with the ♡Q. Zaman now cashed the ♣K and led a club towards dummy. West discarded (the subsequent play is easy if he ruffs) so dummy won the ♣A and the club exit went to East's ♣J. Declarer ruffed the spade return, cashed the ♡A, and now led and ran the ◇J! When this held, he could now ruff a club, cash the ◇K, ruff a spade to hand (or a heart, if West discarded spades on the club leads), draw the last trump, and cash the thirteenth club for his contract.

An elegantly played hand and a contender for the best-played hand of the tournament, perhaps?

Not quite, since Zaman found this excellent line of play a day early — in the 50p a hundred rubber bridge game on the ferry travelling from England to Belgium.

Still it was a nice piece of skill, and well worth recording.

Cartoon Corner

I'm afraid it's 'Members Only' tonight!

TOP FOR DECLARER

BY MAUREEN DENNISON

Mike Ladbrook, of Surrey, was pleased with this top from a County Pairs event.

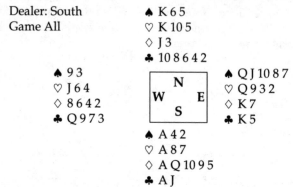

Dealer: South
Game All

♠ K 6 5
♡ K 10 5
◇ J 3
♣ 10 8 6 4 2

♠ 9 3
♡ J 6 4
◇ 8 6 4 2
♣ Q 9 7 3

♠ Q J 10 8 7
♡ Q 9 3 2
◇ K 7
♣ K 5

♠ A 4 2
♡ A 8 7
◇ A Q 10 9 5
♣ A J

Against Ladbrook's 3NT West led the ♣3 to the ♣K and ♣A, and declarer immediately returned the ♣J. Had West ducked, he would have saved a trick for his side but he took his ♣Q — and that was the last trick for his side! He now switched to a diamond, to the ◇K and ◇A, and declarer cashed five tricks in the suit. This was the position:

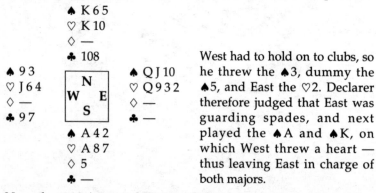

♠ K 6 5
♡ K 10
◇ —
♣ 10 8

♠ 9 3
♡ J 6 4
◇ —
♣ 9 7

♠ Q J 10
♡ Q 9 3 2
◇ —
♣ —

♠ A 4 2
♡ A 8 7
◇ 5
♣ —

West had to hold on to clubs, so he threw the ♠3, dummy the ♠5, and East the ♡2. Declarer therefore judged that East was guarding spades, and next played the ♠A and ♠K, on which West threw a heart — thus leaving East in charge of both majors.

Now the ♣10 squeezed East, and declarer emerged with twelve tricks.

THE SWINDLE

BY CHRIS KINLOCH

Playing in a one-day green-point teams-of-four event where you are in contention, you face the following problem as South, declarer in 4♠:

♠ 5 2
♡ A K 6 4 2
◇ 6 3
♣ A Q 8 5

```
    N
W       E
    S
```

♠ A J 9 8 3
♡ 8 2
◇ Q J 4
♣ K J 6

West, who overcalled in diamonds during the auction, kicks off with ◇ A-K, then switches to a club.

As you cannot afford to lose more than one trick in the trump suit, you must play for a 3-3 break, so you win in dummy planning to finesse the ♠8 next. On the ♠2, however, East plays the ♠K, which you win with your ♠A. You then re-enter dummy with a top heart and lead another spade; East plays the ♠7. What now? Do you play the ♠J or the ♠8? As it is Game All, quite a few IMPs ride on your decision.

Did you reason that East's play might be a wise move if he held ♠K-Q-7? If so, presumably you would play the ♠J so as not to lose to West's ♠10 — and you would go down, since East was indeed false-carding, but from an original holding of ♠K-10-7.

A nice swindle, you say? Well, not quite. The truth is that on this deal you were really supposed to be East who, at the table, played low on the first round of trumps — so declarer finessed the ♠8 and made the contract. However, since at the end of play it was East himself who first thought of the false-card, he'll know what to do next time he is dealt K-10-x, and a small card is led from dummy!

AN ELEGANT IMP

BY SID ISMAIL

Do overtricks matter at teams? The pleasure of gaining them certainly contributes to one's enjoyment of bridge.

Playing in a teams-of-four match, I am South, declarer in 3NT:

♠ 5 3
♡ 10 6 3 2
◇ Q 10
♣ K 9 5 3 2

```
    N
W       E
    S
```

♠ A 9 2
♡ K Q 4
◇ A K 9 3
♣ A Q 6

I receive the lead of the ♠Q, and this seems to be the only lead to give me a problem since there is no time to establish a heart trick. Also, to make nine tricks I have to assume that the clubs behave.

East puts the ♠K on the ♠Q lead and I let her hold this trick. If the spades are 5-3 and the clubs do not come in, I have to play hearts twice from dummy and hope that the ♡A is with East.

Surprise, surprise — East switches to a heart at trick two. So East does not have another spade! I play the ♡K and it holds. Now I lead a diamond to the ◇Q and another heart from table, and the ♡A goes up, West following suit. East plays a third heart to my ♡, and West shows out. Nine tricks are now there irrespective of the club break. How do you continue? The position is shown at the top of the next page.

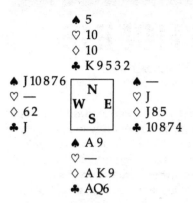

```
              ♠ 5
              ♡ 10
              ◇ 10
              ♣ K 9 5 3 2
♠ J 10 8 7 6            ♠ —
♡ —          N         ♡ J
◇ 6 2      W   E       ◇ J 8 5
♣ J          S         ♣ 10 8 7 4
              ♠ A 9
              ♡ —
              ◇ A K 9
              ♣ A Q 6
```

The ♠A inflicts a triple squeeze on East. If East discards a heart, play the ♣A, ♣Q, and small to the ♣K, then the master heart. East is squeezed again in clubs and diamonds, netting you +660.

A diamond discard from East gives you an extra diamond trick, but there is no further squeeze when you play off the diamonds since you have to discard from dummy before East. This gives you only +630.

Finally, a club discard gives you the club suit, again for +660. At the table, East discarded a club hoping that her partner had two honours in the suit.

In the other room, the play to the first two tricks was the same, but then declarer promptly played four rounds of clubs establishing the suit for a score of +630 — losing the ♠K, ♡A and ♣10.

Thus my squeeze gained us only 1 IMP — but it gave me a lot of pleasure!

A SLIM HOPE

BY MIKE SWANSON

When I am filling in as the spare player on one of my Diamond Bridge Holidays, I always play whatever system my partner feels most comfortable with.

I always hope for a simple system since complicated conventions usually lead to disaster. However, there are a few conventions without which I feel as if I am playing with one hand tied behind my back.

When a recent partner came out with the statement 'I don't play fourth-suit forcing. I have found it never comes up,' I felt that fate was being tempted and, sure enough, I was soon confronted with a bidding problem that had no solution.

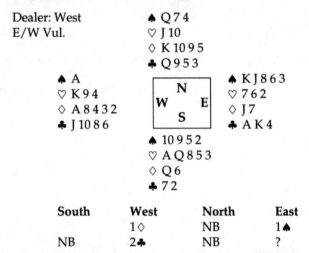

Dealer: West
E/W Vul.

	♠ Q 7 4	
	♡ J 10	
	◇ K 10 9 5	
	♣ Q 9 5 3	

♠ A		♠ K J 8 6 3
♡ K 9 4	N	♡ 7 6 2
◇ A 8 4 3 2	W E	◇ J 7
♣ J 10 8 6	S	♣ A K 4

	♠ 10 9 5 2	
	♡ A Q 8 5 3	
	◇ Q 6	
	♣ 7 2	

South	West	North	East
	1◇	NB	1♠
NB	2♣	NB	?

As East I wanted to bid the fourth suit to say, 'Partner, I know we should be going further, but I have nothing clear-cut to bid at this stage.' However, we had agreed that 2♡ would be a natural call, so I had to come up with an alternative.

Both 2♠ and 3♠ would have been non-forcing (and would have promised a six-card suit), and to bid clubs or diamonds certainly did not look right, so eventually I just closed my eyes, crossed my fingers, and bid 3NT.

South led the ♡5, which I ducked in the dummy. North returned another round of hearts and South, with no outside entry, allowed the dummy to win the trick.

I could now see two spade tricks, one heart trick, one diamond trick and two club tricks, so I had to find three extra tricks from somewhere without letting South win a trick. The club finesse was the obvious source of one, and the spade suit seemed the most sensible hope for more; after all, I just needed North to hold ♠Q-x-x!

Pursuing this slim hope, I cashed the ♠A, took the club finesse, and then played the ♠K and a small spade. When North emerged with the holding I was hoping for, I was home and dry.

In the post-mortem South berated her partner for not defeating the contract. Before reading on, can you see what he could have done to defeat me?

If on the second round of spades North had played his queen, it would have given South the vital entry in the spade suit with her ♠10, so that she could get in to cash her hearts.

However, since we were playing duplicate pairs, where overtricks can make such a difference, I don't think that North could be criticised for not throwing away his ♠Q. At rubber or teams, though, I would expect that many strong players might well find the winning line.

Would you?

EAVESDROPPINGS

After losing a league-of-eight match, the team captain said proudly: 'This is the first time I've bid three grand slams in one match!'

'What's even more remarkable,' replied a team-mate, 'is that one actually made!'

A GAME OF SKILL?

BY RODNEY McCOMBE

It's up to the Editor to choose titles — I would have liked 'A Chapter of Accidents' for this story, but I fear that 'Comedy of Errors' is more appropriate.

Non-vulnerable, my partner sitting North deals and opens 1♡. I hold:

♠ 8
♡ 8
◇ A 8 6 5 3 2
♣ 8 6 4 3 2

I decide to chance a quick 2◇ and hope that no-one will notice. Of course, the roof falls in with a 4♣ ace-enquiry from partner. I should lie and say 'none,' but George Washington would have been proud of my 4♡ reply.

Partner gets cold feet and signs off in 4NT, and I consider the bleak future. Probably five or six down in no-trumps, perhaps only two or three down in diamonds, and it is my fault anyway — why condemn partner to suffer — so I bid 5◇. Partner polishes me off with 6◇!

Now, to be fair, partner *does* have a nice hand, and at least I can hide mine:

♠ A K 10
♡ K J 10 5 3
◇ J 9 7
♣ A K

♠ 8
♡ 8
◇ A 8 6 5 3 2
♣ 8 6 4 3 2

West can hardly be blamed for not finding the heart lead and leads a spade, so the ♠A takes care of my ♠8, and the ♠K of my ♡8.

Let's see how many trumps I will lose by leading the ◇J: ◇Q from East, ◇A from hand and — bang — down comes the ◇K from West. (Is the moral 'never cover an honour with an honour?')

Lead back to the ◊9 which loses to the ◊10 with East, who obliges with the lead of another spade. Ruff in hand, take out the last trump with dummy's ◊7, and lead a small heart.

East needs only one more trick, so goes up with the ♡A, trumped in hand. A club to the ace, then the ♡K followed by a small heart to my last trump fells the ♡Q from West. A club to the king, and the hearts are high. The full deal was:

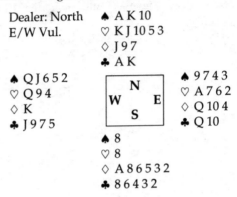

Dealer: North
E/W Vul.

```
                   ♠ A K 10
                   ♡ K J 10 5 3
                   ◊ J 9 7
                   ♣ A K
 ♠ Q J 6 5 2                        ♠ 9 7 4 3
 ♡ Q 9 4            N               ♡ A 7 6 2
 ◊ K           W         E          ◊ Q 10 4
 ♣ J 9 7 5          S               ♣ Q 10
                   ♠ 8
                   ♡ 8
                   ◊ A 8 6 5 3 2
                   ♣ 8 6 4 3 2
```

6◊ made on a combined 23-count — and yet the story would not be worth telling were it not for all the sensible Souths who passed 1♡, and (in a few incredible cases) watched it go one off!

Who says that bridge is a game of skill, in which luck should play no part?

ANONYMOUS QUOTES

'The road to hell is paved with good conventions.'

West Sussex Bridge Club's Newsletter

A FLAT BOARD

BY PETE WATERMAN

This hand occurred nearly twenty years ago in an Open League match between Sheffield University and the Ladies' Club:

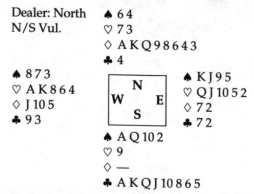

Dealer: North
N/S Vul.

North
♠ 6 4
♡ 7 3
◇ A K Q 9 8 6 4 3
♣ 4

West
♠ 8 7 3
♡ A K 8 6 4
◇ J 10 5
♣ 9 3

East
♠ K J 9 5
♡ Q J 10 5 2
◇ 7 2
♣ 7 2

South
♠ A Q 10 2
♡ 9
◇ —
♣ A K Q J 10 8 6 5

With the University North-South, North opened a 'gambling' 3NT, showing a solid minor suit with nothing outside. I was South and thought: 'I've only got one loser, but I can't use my partner's diamonds unless they are trumps.' I bid 6◇.

I felt OK when the ♡A was led, but on the ♡K continuation I realised the flaw in my reasoning as I struggled in vain to find a trump in my hand. 'Sorry, Dennis,' I said to my partner as I discarded a club for one down.

At the other table, North opened 2◇ and South bid 6♣ on her own after a few rounds of bidding. West, Paul Bowyer, a future International, led the ♡A and, deducing from his partner's signal that there were no more hearts to be cashed, could see that if South had a diamond, a diamond switch would restrict her to one diamond trick (the second round being ruffed by East) instead of eight. Accordingly, he switched to the ◇J. South played the ◇A and ◇K, two spades going away, and then — the ◇Q! This was ruffed by East and overruffed by South.

South could no longer take the spade finesse, so that was one down for a flat board.

HOW COULD WE HAVE DONE BETTER?

BY NEVENA DELEVA

Playing Pairs you hold the West hand below with East-West vulnerable, and the bidding goes:

	South	West	North	East
♠ 10 8 5 3		NB	NB	1♠
♡ 8 2	2♡	2♠	NB	NB
◊ K 10 4	3♡	3♠	4♡	NB
♣ K 9 8 3	NB	Dbl	End	

Opponents play intermediate jump overcalls, therefore it is impossible that a hand which was not worth a jump overcall on the first round of bidding could make a game facing a twice-passed partner. You might be making 3♠ (game is not certain, as you play Acol with a strong no-trump, so apparently partner has an 11-14 balanced hand with four or five spades) and it is easier to get a good score just by doubling, instead of trying to get 4♡ three off.

You lead your fourth-highest spade, and dummy comes down with:

Dummy
♠ J 2
♡ K 10
◊ Q J 7 5
♣ Q J 7 5 2

You
♠ 10 8 5 3
♡ 8 2
◊ K 10 4
♣ K 9 8 3

```
        N
    W       E
        S
```

Dummy plays the ♠2, partner the ♠Q, and declarer wins with the ♠A and returns the ♠9. East wins with the ♠K, and plays the ♣A. Hoping for a diamond switch, you discourage clubs by playing the ♣3 but partner continues with a club to your king. Plan the defence.

Having won the club continuation with the ♣K, I found myself
in a complete-guess situation and had to consider all possibilities.
If declarer had three spades, a spade switch would be the best
one, while any other suit could have given the contract. The
problem was what to do in case declarer had only two spades. I
decided that a spade would still be the best choice, since it would
not cost a trick if South held only six trumps, and, if South had
seven of them, it would be wrong only if partner had the ◇A. (If
South held this card, together with seven trumps, the contract was
solid at this stage.)

Unfortunately, this was the full deal:

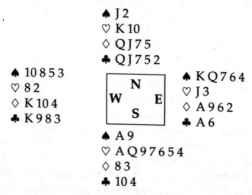

```
                    ♠ J 2
                    ♡ K 10
                    ◇ Q J 7 5
                    ♣ Q J 7 5 2
  ♠ 10 8 5 3              ♠ K Q 7 6 4
  ♡ 8 2          N        ♡ J 3
  ◇ K 10 4    W     E     ◇ A 9 6 2
  ♣ K 9 8 3       S       ♣ A 6
                    ♠ A 9
                    ♡ A Q 9 7 6 5 4
                    ◇ 8 3
                    ♣ 10 4
```

Declarer ruffed the third spade in hand, drew trumps finishing in
dummy, and discarded the losing diamonds on the winning clubs.
As you may guess, minus 590 got us zero match-points, while plus
300 would have been a complete top.

How could we have done better? Obviously, partner was wrong
not to cash the ◇A before playing the second club. If we were going
to score a second club trick, the ◇A would have been the fourth for
the defence, and it couldn't be wrong to cash the setting trick.
Partner had also missed the opportunity to make things easier for
me, during the bidding, when she failed to double 4♡. Had she
done so, I would have known that she must have either the ◇A or
the ♡A at the critical moment for the defence.

I blame myself for two things.

The first one is the opening lead. Although it seems fairly normal
to lead a spade, there is an old golden rule which says that when the
opposition is known not to have enough high-card-point strength

for the contract, and you have stoppers in the side suits, you should lead a trump. The spade lead did not cost on this particular deal, but theoretically it was not the right start and, had I led a heart, we would not have got into such a mess.

The second thing is my signal on partner's ♣A. In this partnership we had agreed to give count most of the time. Although it looked to me like a clear-cut 'attitude' situation, I should have played the ♣9, instead of a low one. Signalling with the ♣3 may well have led partner to think that I had three clubs, and, for my double, two of the three missing high cards (the ♣K, ♢K, and ♡A) which would ensure a club ruff.

Although cashing the ♢A is still the right action at that particular moment in the play, had I played the ♣9 partner would have known that I had four clubs, so she would have realised that the ruff was impossible and she would have tried another defensive option.

Cartoon Corner

Remember, darling, it was you who wanted a team of four!

RUFF TREATMENT

BY MIKE WHITTAKER

Whenever anyone gives you a bridge hand with the question, 'How would you play this ...?' the chances are that you will fail the test. Take this hand, for example — but beware the sting in the tail:

♠ 3
♡ A Q 4
◇ Q 10 8 7 2
♣ A 10 6 5

♠ Q 7 5
♡ K 7 6 3 2
◇ —
♣ K Q 9 7 2

Playing teams, you, South, are in 4♡ after East has overcalled your partner's 1◇ opening bid with 1♠. West leads the ♠2; East wins with the ace and then switches to the ◇A. You to play.

How are you getting on? Partner can't bid, you've missed a slam, and the wrong suit is trumps. OK, ruff the diamond, ruff a spade, play the two top trumps in dummy, back to hand with a club, ♡K, then run the clubs. Ten or eleven tricks, thank you very much, even if the hearts are 4-1. What's the problem?

Was that your line of play? Oh, dear! In the process of returning to hand with a club, East decides to ruff. A spade to West's king and a club return, ruffed again by East, puts you one down.

I know, I know. How unlucky can you get? East has four trumps, a club void, and West has an entry in the ♠K. It's a joke.

The following week the regulars are busy telling their 'can you *believe* what happened to me on this one' stories. Time to bring out the hand above. 'How would you play this in 4♡?' They all go down and are hugely amused by your slice of dreadful luck. And then ...

'You should have thrown a spade at trick two. Now East can never get West in to lead a second club.'

This, I can tell you, is the sort of remark that all storytellers find most unwelcome. I told you there was a sting in the tale.

THE LEYHILL PRISON SWISS TEAMS

BY SUE MAXWELL

L eyhill Prison, which is affiliated to the English Bridge Union, holds a duplicate evening every Friday and, once a year, an Open Swiss Teams. A remarkably popular event, this year it attracted forty-four teams, the organisers having to turn away fifteen teams because of lack of space. Over £1,000 was raised for local charities, and the prizes for the winners are made by the inmates.

Alan Williams, a member of the winning team and also General Manager of the EBU, was held for questioning and very nearly detained after getting away with this one:

Dealer: East
N/S Vul.

	♠ KQJ63	
	♡ 942	
	◇ 82	
	♣ 1054	
♠ 10987		♠ A5
♡ Q107	N	♡ K865
◇ 64	W E	◇ 107
♣ AQ93	S	♣ KJ862
	♠ 42	
	♡ AJ3	
	◇ AKQJ953	
	♣ 7	

South	West	North	East
			1♣
1◇	1♠	NB	2♣
3◇	NB	3NT !!!	End

On the lead of the ♠A, East was sufficiently excited by partner's ♠7 and North's sly honour (the jack) to continue with the suit. North took the next ten tricks.

Can't think why they let him out!

BAD BREAK GOOD (SOMETIMES)

BY TONY PARKINSON

There are two conventional tenets of bridge that one quickly learns in the hurly-burly of competitive duplicate. Generally speaking, if you can't ruff something with the short trump hand, then you are usually better off in a no-trump contract; and if you encounter a really bad break, you may have no recourse in a trump contract either because you've suffered a ruff, or someone still has a winning trump which you can't deal with.

Just to show that this is not always true, consider the following hand from a local league-of-four match — typical end-of-season affair: both teams might still win the league, or be relegated; well, maybe I exaggerate, but you get the drift. The North-South hands were:

♠ A J
♡ A K 5 2
◇ A Q 10 3
♣ A K 6

```
    N
W       E
    S
```

♠ K Q 7 6 2
♡ 6
◇ J 9 5   So do you want to be in 6♠ or 6NT or
♣ 8 7 4 2   neither?

If the spades are 3-3, then you can overtake the ♠J and make twelve or thirteen tricks depending on the diamond finesse, in either spades or no-trumps.

If the spades are 4-2, then you can cash the ♠A and ♠J, then enter the South hand, either via a heart ruff in a spade contract, or by forcing an entry with the ◇J-9 in no-trumps. So you may make thirteen tricks in spades if the diamond finesse works, but can only ever make twelve in no-trumps.

At the table I was South playing in spades, so I won the initial club lead and then cashed the ♠A and ♠J, whereupon East declined to follow to the second round. Now I had an inescapable spade loser, so I needed the diamond finesse to work. The ♡A was cashed and a heart successfully ruffed. The ◇9 was run — and it held. I continued with the ◇J; this also held, and a third diamond to the queen showed that West held four diamonds. Hence I could now cash the ◇A and the ♡K, discarding the two losing clubs, and then play the ♣K. The fact that West ruffed this was immaterial, since I now had the king and queen of trumps to take care of the last two tricks.

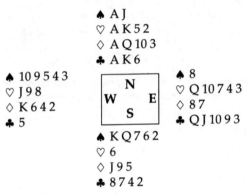

As you can see, with the spades 5-1, the no-trump slam has no play, so the tenets are confounded, and this was obviously a rare triumph for good (that's us of course) over bad (otherwise the opposition). Well, not exactly — I failed to mention the bidding, where we had reached the stratospheric level of 7♠, so it was minus 100 for a flat board.

Sorry, what do I mean 'a flat board'? The opposition had sensibly subsided in 3NT, so that the eventual damage was 13 IMPs.

The bidding? Well, I don't think that descriptions of my systemic deficiencies will enhance the sum of human knowledge, so I believe it should be allowed to remain in the dark.

We lost the match — you might think that I, at least, deserved to.

NEVER GIVE UP

BY BERNARD BRIGHTON

From time to time the post brings me a letter from Canada containing bridge news. The following hand played by Frank Trovato in London, Ontario, quite tickled my fancy. As South, he held:

♠ 5	and opened 1♣. North replied 1♠. Wanting
♡ A Q 2	to show some strength without jumping to
◊ 10 9 6 3	3♣ and needing room to explore 3NT if that
♣ A K Q 7 4	was where the partnership belonged, South
	made a reverse bid of 2◊.

The bad news was that North thought he had a strong hand, too, so before long South found himself the declarer in 6◊. West led a small heart and this is what Frank Trovato saw:

♠ A J 7 6 4 3
♡ K 10
◊ A 8 5 2
♣ 6

♠ 5	The side suits looked solid, but with K-Q-J
♡ A Q 2	missing in the trump suit it seemed obvious
◊ 10 9 6 3	that two diamonds would have to be lost
♣ A K Q 7 4	and the contract would be one down — or
	would it?

Trying to make the best of a bad situation, after winning the heart on table South led to the ♣A, and then ruffed a low club in dummy so as to establish the club suit, whereupon East, perhaps concentrating too hard, followed with a low trump thinking that trumps had been led. The Tournament Director ruled that East's ◊7 had to stay out as a penalty card.

This was good news: it now looked as though South had a ghost of a chance, especially if West could be relied upon to be as fast asleep as East. So declarer switched gear and went for the kill.

After crossing to hand with the ♡A, he led the ◊10 on which West (who had indeed forgotten all about East's penalty card) played low; the ◊2 was played from dummy, and East had to play the ◊7. When another diamond was led to the ace at the next trick, it was delightful to see the ◊J and ◊Q both drop.

A third round of trumps drove out the ◊K, and declarer was home. Who would have thought at the start of the hand that there was any chance at all, no matter how badly the defence played?

Was it Napoleon who said that he would rather have a lucky general on his side than a good one? One day, reflected Frank Trovato, he too would meet his Waterloo — but for now he just got himself an outright top!

Cartoon Corner

She didn't like my forcing pass!

THE DANGER OF OPTIONAL DOUBLES

BY BARRIE PARTRIDGE

A few years ago, I was South on the deal below at a duplicate evening at Matlock Bridge Club:

Dealer: North
E/W Vul.

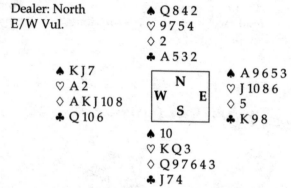

```
                    ♠ Q 8 4 2
                    ♡ 9 7 5 4
                    ◇ 2
                    ♣ A 5 3 2
    ♠ K J 7                          ♠ A 9 6 5 3
    ♡ A 2           N                ♡ J 10 8 6
    ◇ A K J 10 8   W   E             ◇ 5
    ♣ Q 10 6        S                ♣ K 9 8
                    ♠ 10
                    ♡ K Q 3
                    ◇ Q 9 7 6 4 3
                    ♣ J 7 4
```

My partner dealt at favourable vulnerability, and after two passes I took the decision that there may be a spade game against us, so despite being one diamond short I opened 3◇. Our opponents were an established partnership who were playing the 'Optional' Doubles that were quite popular at the time, before the English Bridge Union issued a directive that the word 'optional' by itself was an inadequate description of the call.

Certainly this type of double was not suited for the above deal, but West doubled. Thereafter the auction proceeded:

South	West	North	East
		NB	NB
3◇	Dbl	NB	4◇
NB	4NT	NB	5◇
NB	5NT	NB	6◇
NB	NB	NB	

The 4◇ bid was a forcing take-out bid, and West did take out into 4NT — after all, she had a reasonable stop in diamonds! East thought that 4NT was Blackwood and responded 5◇, showing one ace. As I passed, West was beginning to look confused. Why had her partner bid diamonds twice? If he had diamonds, what did South's opening bid mean?

Now West launched into an interrogation of my partner over my opening bid of 3◇. Eventually, partner was allowed off the witness stand and West settled for a final contract of 5NT. North passed, and East — of course — bid 6◇ to show one king.

I passed. West was now out of her depth. If her partner wanted to bid diamonds three times, he could play in them. After all, it was her best suit!

My partner was highly amused by the proceedings, but kept his head and also passed. The 6◇ contract did not go many off, but enough to give our side a top score. Have you ever pre-empted and then ended up defending against a slam in your suit?

After the play of the hand, East called the Tournament Director to report my 'psychic' opening bid, but he received little sympathy. The Director was my partner!

PLAYING FAST AND LOSE

It is clear from careful observation (the quick player has plenty of time to observe) that in a session of twenty-six boards, two boards a round, the quick player has some five minutes to wait per round, giving a total waiting time over the evening of 13 x 5 = 65 minutes. This, in a total time of, say three and a half hours, is a considerable portion of the evening. Should, then, the fast player pay a third less table money?

N.C.B.A. Newsletter

BETTER BRIDGE

*O*f course **you** would never make any of the errors related in the earlier parts of this book — but are you sure you'd know how to bring off some of the coups described by our authors? If in doubt, read on: this section brings you tips and advice from some of the world's best-known experts.

SIDE SUIT FIRST

BY ROBERT SHEEHAN

When you have a long side suit to be established and a trump position which is at all shaky, it is often best to play on the side suit before drawing trumps. This hand, from a pairs event, illustrates the theme.

Love All
Dealer: East

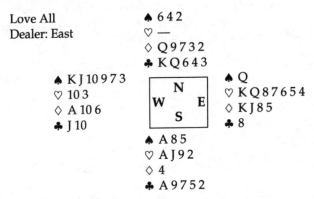

```
                    ♠ 6 4 2
                    ♡ —
                    ◊ Q 9 7 3 2
                    ♣ K Q 6 4 3
  ♠ K J 10 9 7 3          N          ♠ Q
  ♡ 10 3            W         E      ♡ K Q 8 7 6 5 4
  ◊ A 10 6              S             ◊ K J 8 5
  ♣ J 10                              ♣ 8
                    ♠ A 8 5
                    ♡ A J 9 2
                    ◊ 4
                    ♣ A 9 7 5 2
```

Contract: 5♣ by South. Lead: ♣J.

At some tables East opened 3♡, and when South was playing double for penalties (not greatly used nowadays) the final contract was 3♡ doubled. The normal play in the heart suit, with no other indications, is to lead towards the king. However, with the likelihood that South has all the hearts, East can restrict him to two tricks if he starts by leading low towards the ten. That way East makes nine tricks if South doesn't find his diamond ruff.

Some Souths played in 5♣, and received the best lead of a trump. You might think that with ten trumps between the hands it does no harm to draw a second round, but if you did that you are guilty of the fundamental mistake of not counting your tricks. Say you win the second trump in dummy, and belatedly play a diamond. The defence will switch to hearts or spades, and though

101

after each ruff in dummy you can ruff a diamond in hand, by the time the fifth round is established you have no way back to dummy.

The correct technique is to count your tricks: five trumps in hand, two aces and three ruffs — ten tricks in all. To make eleven you have to establish the diamonds, and the way to do that is to play a diamond at trick two. Then if West wins and continues trumps to thwart your cross-ruff plan, you win the trump in dummy. Now you are in the right hand to establish the diamonds — after ruffing a diamond you cash the major suit aces and eventually at the end of the cross-ruff the fifth diamond becomes established and you are in dummy to cash it.

This is a more extreme example, with trump control an important element. It was played in the 1995 American Life Master Pairs. East was the dealer with North-South vulnerable.

♠ A K Q 3
♡ J 10 9 7
◇ 8 7 3
♣ K 8

```
      N
  W       E
      S
```

♠ 8 5 4 2
♡ —
◇ A Q J 10 9 6 4 2
♣ A

South	West	North	East
			NB
1◇	1♡	Dbl*	2♡
4♠	5♣	6♠	End

*Guarantees 4 spades

Contract: 6♠ by South. Lead: ♡8.

South's 4♠ bid looks absurd to me, even at Pairs. A forcing attack is too likely to lead to entry problems. Better to bid 5◇ over 2♡, though whether North would have raised to 6◇ isn't clear. East plays the ♡Q on dummy's jack.

Plan your play before reading on.

This was the full deal:

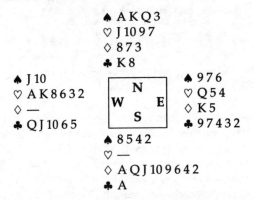

At the table West (Peter Weichsel, playing with Zia Mahmood) led the ♡8, trying to put his partner in for a diamond ruff. South ruffed the first heart, drew trumps and then misguessed the diamonds, enabling the defence to take a diamond and two heart tricks.

In the report of the event, South was criticised for not deducing that West had underled the ♡A — East's play of the queen at trick one surely denied the ace. If South had realised that, it would have led him to the right conclusion about the diamonds.

However, the hand is virtually lay-down if the trumps are 3-2. (If the trumps are 4-1 the hand is unmanageable.) All the declarer has to do after ruffing the heart is cross to dummy with a spade and lead a diamond, finessing when East plays the ♢5. Whether West wins with the singleton king or ruffs, declarer is now in control to take another heart ruff in hand, draw trumps and run the diamonds.

THE POINT OF THE HAND

BY BENITO GAROZZO

When you analyse a hand, the most difficult thing to do is to understand exactly what the problem is. In order to do that, you need to be able to ask yourself: which of the opponents' cards are those that really matter? And in whose hand should they be? Once these points have been established, declarer must proceed with appropriate thoroughness, minding his timing.

Consider, for example, the following — relatively simple — hand which bears out the points above:

♠ A Q 7 6
♡ A Q J 7 2
◇ Q
♣ K Q 6

♠ K J 9 3 2
♡ K 10
◇ A J 7 5 4
♣ 4

You are South, the declarer in 6♠, a contract reached with no opposition bidding. West leads the ♡4; you win in hand and then lead a spade to the Ace, on which, to your surprise and disappointment, East discards the ♣7. Plan the play.

Now apply your plan to all four hands, shown overleaf (and be honest: allow for best defence!). How did you fare?

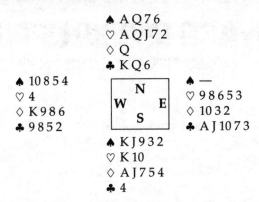

♠ A Q 7 6
♡ A Q J 7 2
◊ Q
♣ K Q 6

♠ 1 0 8 5 4
♡ 4
◊ K 9 8 6
♣ 9 8 5 2

♠ —
♡ 9 8 6 5 3
◊ 1 0 3 2
♣ A J 1 0 7 3

♠ K J 9 3 2
♡ K 1 0
◊ A J 7 5 4
♣ 4

When I was the declarer, I decided that the point of the hand was the location of the ♣A. I further decided that East's ♣7 was strong evidence that it was that defender who held the crucial card. Therefore, without getting involved in adventurous ruffs, I cashed the ◊A and ruffed one diamond, then I played out all the trumps to reach this position:

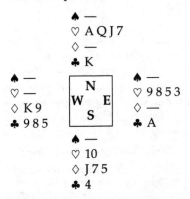

♠ —
♡ A Q J 7
◊ —
♣ K

♠ —
♡ —
◊ K 9
♣ 9 8 5

♠ —
♡ 9 8 5 3
◊ —
♣ A

♠ —
♡ 1 0
◊ J 7 5
♣ 4

When I cashed the ♡10, West discarded a club; I then led my ♣4 to dummy's ♣K. East won with his ace, but then had to lead a heart and put me back in dummy to enjoy my winners.*

*Translated from the Italian by Elena Jeronimidis.

105

BEWARE OVERRUFFING

BY MAUREEN DENNISON

It often pays declarer to look out for opportunities to employ classic defensive manoeuvres, as illustrated by this hand:

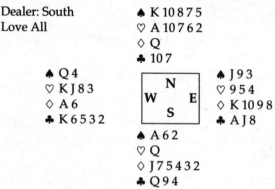

Dealer: South
Love All

♠ K 10 8 7 5
♡ A 10 7 6 2
◇ Q
♣ 10 7

♠ Q 4
♡ K J 8 3
◇ A 6
♣ K 6 5 3 2

N
W   E
S

♠ J 9 3
♡ 9 5 4
◇ K 10 9 8
♣ A J 8

♠ A 6 2
♡ Q
◇ J 7 5 4 3 2
♣ Q 9 4

Junior World Champion Danny Davies, South, opened with a weak 2◇ and there he played. The lead was a club to the ace, and East switched to the ◇K, smothering the queen. He then led the ♣J smothering the ten. Declarer covered, West played the ♣K and then another club which South took with his ♣9. A heart to the ace was followed by a heart ruff, the ♠A-K were cashed, and then declarer ruffed another heart. This was the ending:

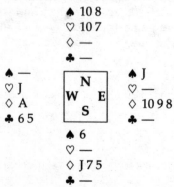

♠ 10 8
♡ 10 7
◇ —
♣ —

♠ —
♡ J
◇ A
♣ 6 5

N
W   E
S

♠ J
♡ —
◇ 10 9 8
♣ —

♠ 6
♡ —
◇ J 7 5
♣ —

Now Davies exited with a diamond and the defence were powerless, whatever West led. If East discarded South would ruff; and if East ruffed, declarer would discard, applying a principle more commonly seen in defence: refusing to overruff can often gain a trump trick. Either way, declarer would make two of the last four tricks and eight tricks in all.

106

THE PRINCIPLE OF ANALOGY

BY TIM BOURKE

Any study of the section on suit combinations in *The Official Encyclopedia of Bridge* is both valuable and daunting. Its merit is that it provides the answers to so many suit-combination problems. Its disadvantage is that it seems to be just a small part of an infinite list of all such combinations.

Alas, unless you are blessed with a photographic memory, it is impossible to remember accurately each and every one of the suit combinations listed in the encyclopædia. The problem would be even worse if all possible combinations were listed. Clearly, what we all want is a technique that enables us to (a) make things easier on the memory, and (b) cope with previously unseen combinations better than we do at present.

Obviously, this article suggests that these requirements can be satisfied and, to make this goal easier to achieve, it will provide you with a basic principle: the *Principle of Analogy*.

Let us begin by considering some of the *key factors*. The things that affect declarer's play in a given suit combination are:

- The number of tricks you need from the suit.

- The number of losers you can afford in the suit.

- The total number of cards held in the suit.

- The suit length in each hand.

- The honours and key pips you have.

- The honours and key pips the defence has.

- The distribution of the honours and key pips in your hand and dummy.

- Entries between dummy and hand — both in and outside the suit.

- Whether the bidding or play indicates that the suit might break abnormally.

- Whether there is a need to keep one of the defensive hands off play.

- Whether you would prefer that *they* led the suit and can afford to try and arrange to force them to do so.

One impediment to absorbing and applying these principles is that their degree of importance varies from suit combination to suit combination, and from hand to hand. To those pessimistic of heart, that may suggest that the task of simplifying suit combinations is impossible.

Before you give up, consider these North-South hands (South unchanged throughout):

Example 1	*Example 2*	*Example 3*
♠ A Q J 10	♠ K J 10 9	♠ Q 10 9 8
♡ A 8 5	♡ A 8 5	♡ A 8 5
◊ A 9 6	◊ A 9 6	◊ A 9 6
♣ K Q 5	♣ K Q 5	♣ K Q 5

N		N		N	
W E		W E		W E	
S		S		S	

♠ 7 5 4	♠ 7 5 4	♠ 7 5 4
♡ K Q 6	♡ K Q 6	♡ K Q 6
◊ K 8 3	◊ K 8 3	◊ K 8 3
♣ A J 10 3	♣ A J 10 3	♣ A J 10 3

In *Example 1*, if West has the ♠K, you will take thirteen tricks by taking repeated spade finesses. Similarly, in *Example 2*, you can take twelve tricks if West has the ♠Q. You do this by leading three times towards North and covering anything West plays, other than the ace, as cheaply as possible.

Example 3 is also quite similar to the previous two. If you were in 5NT you would have to hope that West held the ♠J to make your contract. Your strategy would be to lead repeatedly towards the North hand. You would not play the queen unless West produced the jack.

The thing to observe about the spade suits in the North hand is that they all use the same principle for developing the maximum number of tricks. It suggests that:

If you are unsure how to play a suit combination, try the mental exercise of increasing the rank of the honours in the suit. That exercise may change the combination into one you already know.

This, in a nutshell, is The Principle of Analogy.

For example, consider the North hand in *Example 2*. If you increase the rank of each pip in the spade suit in that hand, it changes into the suit in *Example 1*. The same process can be applied to the third North hand: the first adjustment turns it into the spade suit held by North in *Example 2*, and a second adjustment completes the metamorphosis into the North spade suit in *Example 1*.

While this technique is not invariably accurate, it is an excellent guide in most circumstances. For example, consider the two layouts below:

Combination A	*Combination B*
♠ Q J 4	♠ J 10 4
N W E S	N W E S
♠ A 6 5 2	♠ K 6 5 2

In isolation, the best way of playing for three tricks from *Combination A* is to lead away from the ace twice. Your plan will be to play high from dummy unless West produces the king. Clearly, this plan will yield three tricks when West has the ♠K. If East has this card, your fall-back position is a 3-3 spade break.

In *Combination B*, unless the defence make some useful discards, you can never take more than two tricks in the suit. So, the quest is for two tricks, not three. With such a dramatic lead-in, you should be able to guess how to play *Combination B* for the maximum number of tricks.

That's right! Exactly the same way as you played *Combination A* for three tricks: you lead away from the king twice towards dummy's honours. You work this out by increasing the rank of the honours in the second combination and, presto, it turns into a problem you know how to solve. This is a working example of the Principle of Analogy.

The Principle in Action

Now, here is a case from actual play where declarer applied the Principle of Analogy to the problem involving suit handling:

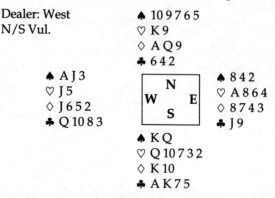

Dealer: West
N/S Vul.

♠ 10 9 7 6 5
♡ K 9
◇ A Q 9
♣ 6 4 2

♠ A J 3
♡ J 5
◇ J 6 5 2
♣ Q 10 8 3

♠ 8 4 2
♡ A 8 6 4
◇ 8 7 4 3
♣ J 9

♠ K Q
♡ Q 10 7 3 2
◇ K 10
♣ A K 7 5

South	West	North	East
	NB	NB	NB
1♡	NB	1♠	NB
2♣	NB	2♡	NB
2NT	NB	3NT	End

West chose the ◇2 for his opening lead.

Declarer took trick one with the ◇10, and decided that playing on hearts first was better than attacking clubs. Now declarer's aim was to play the heart suit for *four* tricks at best (or one loser at worst). The combination in the heart suit was familiar, but not at South's fingertips. However, she dutifully applied the Principle of Analogy, and discovered she could remember the best play for *five* tricks from:

♡ A 10

♡ K J 7 3 2

Namely, low to the ten — even though she could not remember the reasoning behind it. (If the suit breaks 3-3, then it would be a guess as to whom to play for the queen; if someone has a doubleton queen, then she could only pick up five tricks if it were West.)

So, without too much effort, she played a low heart to the nine. Virtue was rewarded when this fetched the ace, and the jack subsequently fell under the king.

110

BEST CHANCES FIRST

BY RON KLINGER

How would you play as South in 3NT on the hands below, after the lead of the ♠3?

♠ K 8
♡ A K 10 7
◇ A K 3
♣ Q J 10 9

```
    N
 W     E
    S
```

♠ 7 6 5
♡ Q 4
◇ Q 9 4 2
♣ A 5 3 2

At the table, declarer went down quickly. He rose with the ♠K in dummy (correct, as the king is doomed unless the ♠A is with West) and took the club finesse (wrong!). This lost to West who cashed four more spades for one off.

Declarer's play would have been right in 6NT, since in that contract four club tricks would be necessary. However, in 3NT, after the ♠K wins, declarer has eight top tricks (one spade, three hearts, three diamonds and one club). Only one more is needed, and that trick could come from diamonds (3-3 break or ◇J-10 doubleton, making the ◇9 high), or from hearts (if the ♡J drops in three rounds), or from clubs (if the finesse works).

On this sort of hand, *you should first take those chances which do not involve losing the lead* (this is known as 'echelon play'). The correct play is: first, cash the three top diamonds; if they behave, you have nine tricks. If not, test hearts playing the ♡Q first, then the ♡A-K; if the ♡J has not dropped, take the club finesse.

When the hand occurred at the table, diamonds split 3-3 so the club finesse was unnecessary.

THE PRINCIPLE OF ANALOGY REVISITED

BY TONY GORDON

Tim Bourke of Australia has written a series of interesting articles on the theme of recognising analogous situations in declarer play. He encapsulates the technique involved in the following Principle of Analogy (*see pages 107-110 of this book*): 'If you are unsure how to play a suit combination, try the mental exercise of increasing the rank of the honours in the suit. That exercise may change the combination into one you already know.'

In this article I am going to use analogous surrounding plays to illustrate how the principle can be adapted to cover defensive situations.

Layout A

$$10\,x\,x$$

$$A\,x\,x \qquad\qquad K\,J\,9\,x$$

$$Q\,x\,x$$

Consider *Layout A* above. If East is declarer and leads the jack intending to finesse the nine on the way back if South covers with the queen, then he is taking a 'backward finesse'. However, if a defender makes this play, he is said to be making a 'surrounding play'. The term arises because the defender's second and third highest cards 'surround' a card on his right. By leading the second highest card, the defender neutralises the power of the surrounded card. In the above layout, leading the nine or the x gives declarer a trick in the suit, whereas leading the jack gives the defence all four tricks. (Leading the king freezes the suit.)

Layout B1 $9\,x\,x$	*Layout B2* $A\,9\,x$
$K\,x\,x \qquad\qquad Q\,10\,8\,x$	$K\,x\,x \qquad\qquad Q\,10\,8\,x$
$A\,J\,x$	$J\,x\,x$

Layout B1 shows one effect of reducing the rank of the key cards by one degree. East must lead the ten to hold declarer to one trick in the suit. It is easily recognisable as being analogous to *Layout A* if North is the dummy, but, as with all surrounding plays, the analogy is not so obvious if the surrounded card is not on view.

Layout B2 shows another effect of reducing the rank of the key cards by one degree, and shows that the concept can be extended to cases where the surrounded card is not the highest card on the defender's right. As in *Layout B1*, East must lead the ten to restrict declarer to one trick in the suit.

Layout C	A 8 x	
Q x x		J 9 7 x
	K 10 x	

Layout C takes the principle one step further and is analogous to *Layout B2*. East must lead the nine to hold declarer to two tricks.

The above examples suggest that the principle we need to use in defence is as follows: 'If you are unsure how to defend against a suit combination, try the mental exercise of increasing the rank of certain cards in the suit in your hand and in the dummy. That exercise may change the combination into one you already know.'

Layout D	A 7 3	
K J 4		10 8 6 5
	Q 9 2	

Layout D occurred in actual play. South was declarer and needed two tricks in the suit, but knew that the king was offside. East was on lead and led the five, but this enabled declarer to play low from hand, and after the jack forced the ace a finesse of the nine on the way back produced a trick for the queen.

It is understandable that East did not recognise this defensive combination, but if he had applied the Defensive Principle of Analogy, he would surely have recognised either *Layout C* or *B2*, and have deduced that the correct lead was the eight.

BASIC HAND EVALUATION

BY DAVID PARRY

One of the first things you learn when you take up bridge is the Milton Work Point Count method of hand evaluation: 4 points for an ace, 3 for a king, 2 for a queen, and 1 for a jack. The scheme is pretty accurate for balanced hands, but is no substitute for good judgement. Usually good judgement comes only with years of experience, but there are several pointers which can be picked up quickly.

Both the following hands contain 14 points, but *Hand A* is distinctly superior to *Hand B*. Before reading on, see if you can list five reasons why.

Hand A	*Hand B*
♠ A K 10 9	♠ K Q
♡ A K 10 9	♡ K Q J
◇ 10 9 8	◇ Q 6 5 4
♣ 3 2	♣ J 6 5 3

1. *Hand A* is packed with intermediate cards — tens and nines. *Hand B* has none.

2. *Hand A* has its points concentrated in the long suits, which enhances its playing strength. Most of *Hand B*'s values are in the short suits.

3. *Hand A* is rich in aces and kings. Aces tend to be slightly undervalued by the point count. *Hand B* has no ace at all and two jacks, and on many hands not all the jacks will play a significant role.

4. *Hand B* has two suits with honours but no small cards. If an opponent leads the ♠A you want to be able to follow with a spot card, not waste a valuable queen. Singleton honours are further examples of poor holdings.

5. *Hand A* has length in the major suits and most importantly spades. If the auction becomes competitive and you have a spade fit you will be able to outbid your opponents without raising the level.

A long suit can be a considerable asset, and the basic (high-card) point count should be adjusted accordingly.

Various systems have been devised. The best is simply to add a point for each card after the fourth in every suit, except when you hold four-card or longer support for partner. Then it is not so much the long suits, but rather the short suits, which add value to your hand because of the ruffing potential they offer; instead you should add 5 points for a void, 3 for a singleton, and 1 for a doubleton. Note that you should not add points for both length and shortage at the same time.

Suppose partner opens with (i) 1♠ or (ii) 1♡. How would you value the following responder's hand?

Responder
♠ 6
♡ A 9 7 6
♢ K Q 10 9 6
♣ J 8 5

(i) Opposite a 1♠ opening, the hand has 11 points, counting 1 for the long diamonds.

(ii) Opposite a 1♡ opening, the hand is worth 13 points including 3 for the singleton spade.

MISUNDERSTANDINGS

Declarer had just taken a trick when LHO exclaimed indignantly. 'That was mine! You took mine!' Confusion followed as declarer tried to explain why she claimed the trick, when finally LHO's voice was heard above the hubbub: 'What I'm trying to tell you,' she stated, glaring at declarer, 'is that you're drinking *my* coffee!'

Nan Haley, ACBL Bulletin

EXCLUSION BLACKWOOD

BY ALLAN FALK

How often have you felt that slam was in the air, but been unable to check on aces because a void in a side suit would have made Blackwood useless? It happens to experts as it does to lesser mortals.

From whatever laboratory it is that develops new bridge conventions, a nice solution has emerged: 'Exclusion Blackwood'. This entails bidding five of your void suit, rather than 4NT, to ask for aces. Partner responds by showing aces in steps (first step = 0 aces), ignoring the ace of the void suit

This basic scheme can, however, be ignored if the occasion demands it. Here is an example from the 1988 Fall North American Championship:

	♠ K 8			♠ A 7 2
	♡ A K J 9 6 2	N		♡ Q 5 4
	◇ K Q 9 6 4	W E		◇ 5 3
	♣ —	S		♣ Q 10 8 4 3

South	West	North	East
	1♡	NB	2♡
3♣	5♣	NB	6♡
End			

West, hearing South announce club values, foresaw safety at the five level even if East had no ace, so he launched into Exclusion Blackwood by bidding 5♣. With one ace, the response should have been 5♡, but with the ♡Q East's hand must be good enough for slam. Rather than risk watching West deliberate over a 5♡ response and then pass, East simply bid what he thought he could make. The ◇A was onside as expected, and South had no more than two trumps, so it was easy and safe to ruff a diamond and claim.

It should be noted that if the trump suit were a minor, a leap to four of a higher-ranking suit, or to 5♣ if the suit were diamonds, would also be Exclusion Blackwood. Further developments of the convention are subject to partnership agreement, as illustrated by this example from the *Bridge World* feature 'Challenge the Champs' (January 1972, Problem 8):

♠ 9			♠ A 10 3
♡ A K 3 2		N	♡ Q 9 8 6 5 4
◇ Q J 10 8	W	E	◇ —
♣ A 8 4 3		S	♣ K Q 10 9

South	West	North	East
	1◇	1♠	2♡
NB	3♠	NB	5◇
NB	5NT	NB	7♡
End			

The auction starts familiarly enough, but on the second round West, on the way to 4♡, with his excellent controls shows his spade shortness with a Splinter Bid of 3♠. East cannot imagine a West hand that does not contain at least one working key card, so 5♡ must be safe, even if the opener has the wasted ◇A-K-Q-J. East's 5◇ is Exclusion Blackwood.

West, having opened the bidding and shown extra values by bidding 3♠, has three key cards outside diamonds (the ♡A, ♣A, and ♡K), and shows them by bidding 5NT (the third step, with 5♡, the first step, showing one). That is all East needs to contract for the grand slam bonus, although in other situations East could now ask for second or third round control in another suit — for example, if he held only ♣K-J-10-9 he could bid 6♣ to ask for the queen.

Do make a note of that twist: when Exclusion Blackwood is in the next lower touching suit, you must have an agreement with partner as to the minimum number of key cards, based on previous bidding, that the responder needs in order to bypass five of the agreed trump suit. Without such an agreement, you might be forced to slam with two controls missing.

A nice tool. Like fire, avoid playing with it! Use sparingly, and profit handsomely.

WHEN IN DOUBT, LEAD TRUMPS (OR DO YOU?)

BY ERIC CROWHURST

Bridge players, in my experience, range from those who, like most beginners at the game, *never* lead trumps, to those who lead trumps far too often, simply because they lack either the courage or the wit to lead anything else. The motto of the second group is the old bromide, 'When in doubt, lead trumps,' but this is, of course, a gross over-simplification. In reality, the correct balance lies somewhere between the two extremes, and you should lead a trump not because you are in doubt, but because you hope to accomplish a specific purpose.

The situations in which the opening leader's fingers should hover over a trump can be summarised as follows:

(a) When it is clear from the bidding that declarer is planning to make ruffing tricks in dummy.

After auctions of this type:

(i)	South	West	North	East
	1♡	NB	1NT	NB
	2♣	End		

(ii)	South	West	North	East
	1♡	NB	1♠	NB
	2◇	End		

It is very likely that dummy will be very short in declarer's first suit. A trump lead therefore sticks out like a sore thumb, particularly if West has a strong holding in declarer's first suit and can expect to make tricks therein once dummy's ruffing value has been removed.

It is important to remember that similar considerations do not necessarily apply if the responder gives preference to the opener's first suit. Thus:

(iii)	South	West	North	East
	1♡	NB	1♠	NB
	2♣	NB	2♡	End

While North might be short of clubs on this auction, this is only a possibility rather than a probability. In fact, North could even have more clubs than hearts, for he should always give 'false preference' if he has 2-3 in his partner's two suits.

(b) When a low-level take-out double has been passed for penalties.

(iv)	South	West	North	East
	1♡	Dbl	End	

East's pass in this situation should be based on a long and fairly solid holding in hearts. Since East might eventually be in a position to extract the declarer's small trumps, an opening trump lead is mandatory.

There is another way of looking at this position. West's double offered his partner a number of possible contracts, but East has effectively chosen to play in 1♡. If East were the declarer, he would be anxious to draw the opponents' small trumps so that he could enjoy all his side-suit winners. West should therefore set this plan into action by leading a heart at trick one.

(c) When the auction has died at the one level and your partner is known to have fair values.

Suppose that you, West, hold this hand:

♠ 10 9
♡ Q 10 4 2
◇ K Q 9
♣ 8 7 6 5

The bidding has gone:

(v)	South	West	North	East
	1♠	End		

East would obviously have bent over backwards to reopen the bidding in the protective position, particularly at match-pointed pairs. You know from North's pass and your modest holding that East must have the wherewithal to bid something; the fact that he has chosen not to suggests that he has a good holding in the opponent's suit and prefers to defend. An opening trump lead might therefore enable East to draw the declarer's small trumps at a later stage.

(d) When dummy has removed a penalty double during the course of the auction.

(vi)	South	West	North	East
	1♠	NB	2♠	3♣
	Dbl	NB	3♠	End

The fact that North has pulled his partner's penalty double of 3♣ strongly suggests that he is very short in the suit. The declarer's line of play in 3♠ will therefore be to ruff his long clubs in dummy, and the defenders should forestall this plan by leading trumps at every opportunity.

(e) When you have five trumps.

Whenever you find yourself in the fortunate position of holding five cards in the opponents' chosen trump suit, you should give serious thought to leading a trump if it appears likely that the opponents are playing in a 4-4 fit. It should be possible for you to retain control of the hand, and drawing two trumps for one by repeated trump leads will reduce the number of tricks which the declarer can make by playing on cross-ruff lines.

There is actually a second potential benefit to be gained from leading trumps when you have five of them. If you fail to remove trumps as quickly as you can, you might find your length in the suit awkward in the end game and you might, for example, find yourself forced to ruff your partner's trick and concede another trick by returning a trump.

(f) When you are defending against a grand slam.

When the opponents have contracted to make all thirteen tricks, every one of them is certain to be precious. The slightest slip by the defenders is likely to be fatal, and you should avoid taking the slightest risk by opening up one of the side suits at trick one. Even if you have K-Q-J-10 in an unbid suit, an original trump lead might still work out better — by reducing the number of trump tricks which the declarer can make separately, or by attacking his entries between the two hands.

*(g) When your side has the balance of the high-card strength and
the opponents' most likely source of tricks is some kind of cross-ruff.*

If it seems likely that the opponents are outgunned in terms of high cards, repeated trump leads will limit the number of tricks available to the declarer. The common situations in which this point is particularly valid are (i) when the opponents are obviously sacrificing after you have bid a contract which you expected to make, and (ii) when you and/or your partner have attempted to play in a no-trump contract, only to be outbid by a determined opponent.

*(h) When your holdings in the opponents' long suits
suggest that declarer will need to play on cross-ruff lines.*

Suppose that you, West, hold this hand:

♠ K J 9 4
♡ J 4
♢ Q J 10 7
♣ K 8 2

The bidding has gone:

(vii)	South	West	North	East
	1♠	NB	2♢	NB
	2♡	NB	3♡	NB
	3NT	NB	4♡	End

West knows that South's spade suit will be difficult to establish. He also knows that dummy's diamonds will not come in and that the ♣K is well placed for the defenders. A substantial proportion of the ten tricks which South requires will therefore have to come from the trump suit, and repeated trump leads by the defenders will keep these to an absolute minimum.

*(i) When the bidding has been unrevealing and your holdings in the side
suits are not attractive.*

Suppose that you hold this hand as West:

♠ 10 5 2
♡ Q 6 4 2
♢ K 7
♣ A 10 6 3

The bidding has gone:

(viii)	South	West	North	East
	1♠	NB	3♠	NB
	4♠	End		

It is not clear from the bidding that an attacking lead is required, and an opening lead from one of the three unattractive side-suit holdings could work out extremely badly. An opening trump lead therefore looks best.

A trump lead of this type is even more strongly recommended when the opponents' hands are both limited. For example:

(ix)	South	West	North	East
	1NT	NB	2♣	NB
	2♠	NB	3♠	NB
	4♠	End		

After such an auction, there is no reason to suspect that a long suit somewhere will provide vital discards. Moreover, both opponents' hands are strictly limited, and they clearly have nothing to spare for their game contract. West should therefore attempt to avoid giving away a trick with the opening lead, and a trump lead will usually be best if West does not have an attractive holding in one of the side suits.

BRIDGE SECRETS FROM THE MASTERS

BY MARK HORTON

Nearly all top players agree that if you want to improve, then you must read and play as often as possible. There is no shortage of books to choose from, but how many of them offer original advice? In recent years the book to make the greatest impact was Larry Cohen's *The Law of Total Tricks*, and even that was based on a known theory.

If you move in the company of experts you find that they are always making original suggestions and comments, but many of them never appear in print and so remain unknown to the vast majority of players. It's high time that situation was remedied!

Let's begin by considering some advice about opening leads against no-trump contracts.

Suppose the bidding goes 1NT — 3NT and you are on lead with:

♠ A 8 6 2	If you decide to lead a major which do you
♡ K 7 5 3	choose? If you remember the standard advice
◇ 8 6 4	of 'fourth best of your longest and strongest'
♣ 9 3	then presumably you will select a spade.

There are several reasons why this is probably wrong.

First of all there is the advice of the Scottish International, the late Tom Culbertson: 'Always lead from the suit where you don't have a certain re-entry.'

Here you can't be certain who has the ♡A and if it turns up in the dummy you may never be able to cash any long spades that leading that suit might establish.

Then there is the remark made by Bob Rowlands when he was given a not dissimilar hand as a lead problem. On being told that the opening lead was a spade he commented: 'I would have led any one of the other suits first!'

The amazing Sharples twins had a theory, based on their many years of playing together, that given any sort of close decision between the lead of a heart or a spade, a heart worked out better.

While you could never get them fully to explain the logic behind this, it seems to work! In Sweden they already seem to know this — take a look at this deal from the Teams Olympiad played in Valkenburg in 1980:

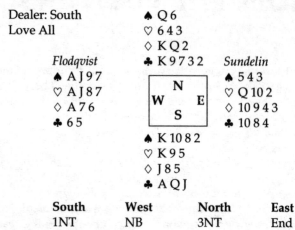

Dealer: South
Love All

♠ Q 6
♡ 6 4 3
◇ K Q 2
♣ K 9 7 3 2

Flodqvist
♠ A J 9 7
♡ A J 8 7
◇ A 7 6
♣ 6 5

Sundelin
♠ 5 4 3
♡ Q 10 2
◇ 10 9 4 3
♣ 10 8 4

♠ K 10 8 2
♡ K 9 5
◇ J 8 5
♣ A Q J

South	West	North	East
1NT	NB	3NT	End

When the opponents don't investigate the possibility of a major suit fit, it is usually a good idea to lead one. With a choice between hearts and spades, should West prefer a spade because they are 'stronger'?

Flodqvist had no doubts: he selected a heart. What is more, he reasoned that with his three aces he could afford to take a look at dummy, and led the ♡A. When 'P.O.' played an encouraging ♡10, he continued with a low heart setting up five tricks for the defence.

On a low spade lead declarer can make 3NT.

You can apply these principles to other combinations. Suppose we change our original example to:

♠ K 8 6 2	This time you have no certain re-entry but
♡ Q 7 5 3	you are more likely to get in with a spade, so
◇ 8 6 4	you lead a heart.
♣ 9 3	

That's enough about no-trump contracts and it's time to listen to some advice from the great Tony Forrester about opening leads against suit contracts.

Forrester made it very clear that the opening lead was one of the most dangerous moments for the defence. Although he would be the first person to make an attacking lead when the bidding called for it, his golden rule was: 'Don't lead away from a king if you have any decent alternative.'

Following this rule will save you a lot of tricks over the years, and you won't often find a deal where a contract which makes could otherwise have been defeated.

Generally speaking, experts don't like leading trumps and the combination of that and Forrester's principle placed two-time World Champion Sally Brock in an interesting situation. She had the following hand:

♠ 6
♡ K 8 7 2
◇ K J 6 3
♣ K 9 5 4

Her opponents had bid 1♠ — 4♠ and it was her lead. Given the restraints (don't lead away from a king and don't lead a trump) she appeared to have an insoluble problem.

If, like Brock, you led a diamond, then go to the top of the class for this was the full deal:

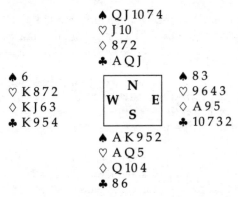

```
                ♠ Q J 10 7 4
                ♡ J 10
                ◇ 8 7 2
                ♣ A Q J
  ♠ 6                         ♠ 8 3
  ♡ K 8 7 2        N          ♡ 9 6 4 3
  ◇ K J 6 3    W     E        ◇ A 9 5
  ♣ K 9 5 4        S          ♣ 10 7 3 2
                ♠ A K 9 5 2
                ♡ A Q 5
                ◇ Q 10 4
                ♣ 8 6
```

Of course she didn't simply close her eyes and hope for the best! She reasoned that if partner held the ◇ Q then leading that suit might set up two tricks, whilst a similar holding in either hearts or clubs would only establish one trick.

Tony Sowter is not only a top class player, he is also one of the best bridge teachers. Here is one of his ideas which will repay careful study.

You are playing in an international team tournament when you pick up the North hand below:

♠ Q 5
♡ K Q 5
◇ K 7
♣ A 8 7 6 4 2

♠ A 10 8 3
♡ A J 10 7 4
◇ 8 6 3   You open 1♣ and partner responds 1♡.
♣ 5   What should you bid?

At the table the rebid was 2♣ which became the final contract.

Even though you have only three-card heart support, your club suit is moth-eaten and you should prefer a rebid of 2♡. As a general rule, you should try and show good support for a suit bid by your partner as soon as possible.

Now we come to the crux of the hand: should South bid on over 2♡? A lot of players would argue that with only nine points a pass is indicated but, as Sowter points out, your hand is worth much more than that!

As soon as your five-card suit has been supported, you can be almost certain that your fifth heart will be a winner. To make it easy to evaluate your hand, think of the extra trick as a king. With 40 high card points in the pack each 'extra' king is worth almost exactly one trick.

Here you have 9 high-card points and one 'extra' king, a total of twelve points. That is enough to bid game, especially at teams. A 4♡ contract isn't lay-down, but the cards were well placed and it made in comfort at the other table.

INFERENCE FROM A PRE-EMPT

BY ANDREW ROBSON

Say you open the bidding with a three-level pre-empt. Soon you find yourself on lead to an enemy trump contract. What do you lead?

Well, of course you need to know your hand, but generally? *A priori*?

Perhaps the first thing that occurs is that you will lead a side-suit singleton, if you have one. How likely is that going to be? We shall assume a fairly aggressive, though sane, style of pre-empting: that, as well as seven-card suits, you will open a fair number of 6-3-3-1 or 6-4-2-1 hand patterns at the three level, but very few 6-3-2-2 or 6-4-3-0 shapes. In this event, your hand will contain a singleton over three-quarters of the time, and if that singleton is in a side suit you will generally lead it.

The enemy have an unfortunate habit, however, of playing in their longest trump fit. Thus, sadly, your singleton is more likely to be in trumps than elsewhere. In fact, about half the time you are on lead to a trump contract, having pre-empted, you will hold a singleton trump. Now what do you tend to lead holding a 7-3-2-1, 6-3-3-1, or 6-4-2-1 shape with a singleton trump? Most of the time you lead your own suit, do you not?

What of the other 20-25% of hands, when you don't hold a singleton at all? On a little under half such deals you will hold a void (7-3-3-0, 7-4-2-0, very occasionally 6-4-3-0) and not surprisingly it will nearly always be in trumps, particularly if partner has doubled! On the rest you will be 7-2-2-2 (or occasionally 6-3-2-2). Again on all these hands you are likely to lead your own suit.

The final conclusion: if a pre-emptor leads his own suit, he will have a singleton trump about two-thirds of the time; but he will have two or more trumps less than one-fifth of the time, basically the dreaded 7-2-2-2 pattern, though actually nearly four times less frequent than the 7-3-2-1. More simply expressed:

The large majority of pre-empts contain a singleton; if it is in a side suit it will be led; if it isn't led, it's in trumps!

With the above in mind, you can improve on my line of play on this hand from the Cap Gemini 1991:

♠ K J 10 4
♡ 6 4
◇ J 8 4 3
♣ K 4 3

	N	
W		E
	S	

♠ A 9 8 3
♡ K Q J 9 5 3
◇ 10 9 2
♣ —

South	West	North	East
Robson	*Kreijns*	*Forrester*	*Tammens*
	3♣	NB	3NT
4♡	End		

When dummy hits the table, you realise that you would have done better to pass or double East's 3NT. But West's lead of the ♣A gives you a chance.

At the table I ruffed, crossed to the ♠K, ditched a diamond on the ♣K, and played a heart to the king. I was essentially playing for both majors to break, with ♠Q doubleton. This was unlikely — virtually impossible after the pre-empt and the 3NT bid. I ended up two down. Let's analyse the clues available. West has found an unattractive ace lead in his pre-empt suit; so where is his singleton? Surely not in diamonds or spades, or he would have led it. Thus it is in trumps. And East, no joker, has bid 3NT — thus he has the guarded ♠Q.

These clues, none of them certain, but all fairly plain if given enough thought, lead to the following line: after crossing to the ♠K and taking your diamond discard on the ♣K, run the ♠J. Assuming it is not covered, play a heart to the ♡9! If the spade is covered, play a top heart from hand to draw West's singleton and subsequently cross to dummy's ♠10 and play a heart to the ♡9.

Neat! Let's hope West's singleton is not the ♡10, as it may well be if East doesn't cover the ♠J. Note that playing East for ♠Q-x-x forces us to play West for a singleton trump (or the ace — impossible on the bidding) otherwise East can rise with the ♡A to give his partner a spade ruff.

The full hand is as expected:

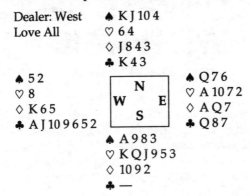

Dealer: West ♠ K J 10 4
Love All ♡ 6 4
◇ J 8 4 3
♣ K 4 3

♠ 5 2   N   ♠ Q 7 6
♡ 8   W   E   ♡ A 10 7 2
◇ K 6 5   S   ◇ A Q 7
♣ A J 10 9 6 5 2   ♣ Q 8 7

♠ A 9 8 3
♡ K Q J 9 5 3
◇ 10 9 2
♣ —

This article was the 1991 runner-up in the prestigious Bols Tips
competition.

What do you understand by your partner's 4   bid?

GOING TO BED WITH A BID

BY PAUL HACKETT

We all have our moments when we fall asleep at the table, going off in cold contracts, forgetting a card, or even revoking. All of these are forgivable by most partners, but there are some cardinal sins which even the most understanding of partners find hard to stomach. Learn to avoid them — for here they are:

1. Bidding our hand twice.

We pick up:

♠ 3	Partner opens with 1♡ and we bid 3♡. Next
♡ K J 7 5 4	hand bids 3♠, and after two passes we bid
◇ K 8 6 4 2	4♡. Opponents now bid 4♠ and it makes.
♣ 7 4	

How many times have we heard the excuse: 'I should have bid 4♡ in the first place'? In that case, bid it, but do not bid 3♡ and then 4♡. If you thought you were only good for 3♡, so be it — but pass at your next turn.

2. Not bidding when we should.

We hold:

♠ A J 6	Partner passes. RHO opens 1♡; we pass but
♡ K J 7 5	come in later, losing 800. 'I didn't bid earlier
◇ A Q 4	because I disliked my clubs and you had
♣ Q 6 5	passed, partner,' we say.

Get the hand off your chest, and bid 1NT at your first turn. If you go for an early penalty, that's unlucky — but the longer you wait, the easier it is for opponents to double.

3. *Not trusting partner.*

We hold:

♠ 6	Partner opens with 1♡ and we bid 4♡. The
♡ K J 7 5 4 2	bidding now proceeds NB — NB — 4♠. We
◇ K 8 6 5	pass, and partner doubles.
♣ 7 4	

Pass. If you bid 5♡ and are doubled, going two down when 4♠ could never make, how will you defend your action?

4. *Passing a forcing bid because we did not have our bid.*

Our hand is:

♠ K 7 2	We open 1♡; partner bids 2♣; we rebid 2NT
♡ A J 6 5 3	(15-16), partner bids 3♡, and we pass.
◇ Q J 4	'Partner, I stretched when I bid 2NT,' one tries
♣ K 7	to explain after wrapping up three overtricks.

If you up-value your hand, carry it through.

X-RATED BRIDGE

A nurse was reading aloud the get-well cards received by a bridge player who had been badly injured in a car crash. One card, from the Chairman of the local bridge club, began like this: 'Dear Lelia, I picked this hand up last night ...' and included a diagram with each small card represented in the usual way by an 'x'.

'Ooh!' said the nurse. 'This one's from a man — and it's full of kisses!'

Audrey Rostron

THE SMITH PETER

BY ANDREW KAMBITES

On the hand below you are playing duplicate pairs, so overtricks matter. Your primary signalling system is to show count, so when declarer takes your ♠Q lead with dummy's ♠A at trick one, East shows count. At trick two the ♡Q is run to your ♡K. This leaves you wondering whether it is safe to continue spades.

```
                    ♠ A 5 3
                    ♡ Q 9 5 3
                    ◇ K 8
                    ♣ K Q J 9

      ♠ Q J 9 4            N
      ♡ K 6           W         E
      ◇ 10 9 6 5 3         S
      ♣ 8 4
```

South	West	North	East
		1♣	NB
1♡	NB	2♡	NB
3NT	NB	4♡	End

Declarer could have either of the following:

Hand A	*Hand B*
♠ 10 8 6	♠ K 10 6
♡ A J 10 4	♡ A J 10 8
◇ A 4 2	◇ J 4
♣ A 10 7	♣ A 10 5 3

If declarer has *Hand A*, you must quickly take your two spades to hold him to ten tricks. But if he has *Hand B*, a spade continuation will be fatal, letting through an unmakeable contract. Does partner have the ♠K which would make a spade continuation safe? He couldn't show you at trick one because you play count signals, but if you play *Smith Peters* he has an opportunity to show you at trick two!

The idea of a Smith Peter is that if declarer or dummy wins trick one, the first card played on declarer's suit at trick two shows attitude towards the suit of the opening lead.

Let us now return to the example hand above. At trick two, East will play a high heart to show that he likes spades — or a low heart to discourage in spades.

Try another example:

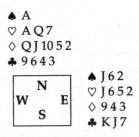

♠ A
♡ A Q 7
◇ Q J 10 5 2
♣ 9 6 4 3

♠ J 6 2
♡ J 6 5 2
◇ 9 4 3
♣ K J 7

Your opponents bid 1NT — 3NT. West leads the ♠K, and dummy's ◇Q is led at trick two. How should you (East) signal to each of these tricks?

On trick one, play the ♠2 to show an odd number of spades. At trick two, play the ◇9 to show that you like spades. Partner's ◇K wins this trick, and he can now confidently continue with a low spade from his original holding of ♠K-Q-10-5-3.

The final example shows that the opening leader can play a Smith Peter to show the strength of his suit:

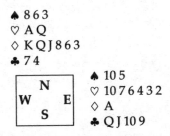

♠ 8 6 3
♡ A Q
◇ K Q J 8 6 3
♣ 7 4

♠ 10 5
♡ 10 7 6 4 3 2
◇ A
♣ Q J 10 9

Once again, your opponents bid 1NT — 3NT. West (your partner) leads the ♠4 to your ♠10 and declarer's ♠J. At trick two you take the ◇A. Do you persevere with spades (essential if West started with ♠A-Q-7-4-2) or do you switch to a club (which is necessary if West has weak spades and the ♣A)?

Watch West's diamond at trick two! A high diamond would show strong spades, while a low diamond would discourage in spades, making the ♣Q switch your only hope.

THINK BEFORE YOU PLAY

BY MORAG MALCOLM

Here is a well-known hand from which you can judge how experienced you are:

♠ K J 4
♡ 4 3
◇ 5 4
♣ K Q J 10 7 6

♠ A 6
♡ A K 7 2
◇ A 8 3 2
♣ 8 4 3

You, South, are declarer in 3NT, and West leads the ♠5. First of all, count your tricks. Two spades, two hearts, one diamond and five clubs add up to ten. Is there a problem? Can you go down?

Yes — easily! If you play the ♠J at trick one and it wins. East holds up the ♣A for two rounds and you have no entry to reach all your club tricks. To make the contract you must *think before you play* — win trick one with the ♠A, and you cannot be defeated.

♠ 7 6 5
♡ K 9 6 4
◇ A J 8 7
♣ A Q

♠ 4 2
♡ A Q J 8 7
◇ K Q 6
♣ 7 5

You are South, in a contract of 4♡, and West leads a small club. Think! Count! You can see five heart tricks, four in diamonds, and one in clubs — which is the ten tricks you need. Is there a problem? Can you go down?

Yes — if you finesse the ♣Q. East may win the ♣K and shoot back a spade, and you might lose three spades to go down. The club finesse is unnecessary. In short — *think before you play!*

NO-TRUMP BIDDING

BY PAUL MENDELSON

It's just one of life's mysteries, isn't it, why 3NT makes with only a combined 22 points (you, at the other table, are in 1NT of course), and then goes down on the next hand with 30 points?

Actually, I think that there isn't quite as much mystery as you might think. It is simply that many players who busily undertake radical computations of point-adjustment for hand valuation, together with losing, combined, and total tricks for a trump contract, shut their eyes and use their fingers for no-trumps.

The construction of the hand is vital for success in no-trumps. In simple words, aces and kings are overrated; queens, jacks, tens and nines are worth more than their usual values. Old-fashioned it may be, but I think that you should count half a point for a ten, and definitely add one point if you have a five-card suit. Seen in this light, the following hands may be worth more (or less) than you might usually think:

Hand A	Hand B	Hand C
♠ A 4 3	♠ Q J 9	♠ K J 8
♡ A 5 4 3	♡ Q 9	♡ Q J 7
◇ A 4 2	◇ K 10 9 8 7	◇ Q J 10 9 8
♣ Q 5 2	♣ K 10 3	♣ A 10

Hand A looks like a maximum for a 12-14 1NT, but the construction is all wrong — all aces and no undergrowth. If partner raised me to 2NT, I would think twice before bidding 3NT.

Hand B has only 11 points, so obviously we cannot open 1NT — oh yes we can! It has two tens (that's worth another point) and a five-card suit. This hand is worth at least 13 points in no-trumps, and you should open with 1NT in any position or vulnerability. If partner bids 2NT, you might even try 3NT playing rubber or teams. At Pairs, you may have done well enough playing in no-trumps, or not throwing in the hand.

Hand C is not a maximum 1NT opener. It is not a 1NT opener at all! It is far too good. You should open 1◇ and rebid 1NT to show 15-16 points.

What about *Hand D*?

Hand D
- ♠ 8
- ♡ Q J 9 8
- ◇ K 10 9 8
- ♣ A Q J 7

I've written before now that 4-4-4-1 hands with 12 or 13 points are usually best passed, and generally I stick to that and reap the rewards.

However, when the 13 points are this good, I can't resist entering the fray. I don't care for any of the suit possibilities — I play that bidding two suits always promises least a 5-4 distribution — so what about 1NT?

I know that this is something of a rogue suggestion, but what can go wrong? We'll find our 4-4 heart fit with Stayman, we won't play in a spade game unless partner has six and, if we end up in 3NT, we'll have the opponents confused.

If you talk about this with a regular partner, you must disclose it on your convention card, otherwise it is an illegal partnership understanding. If you are a cut-in rubber bridge player, keep it to yourself. You wouldn't want your opponents adopting your style.

Such principles equally apply to the responder. Your partner opens 1NT (12-14, of course). What do you respond on each of these hands?

Hand E	*Hand F*	*Hand G*
♠ A 4 3	♠ Q J 9	♠ 8
♡ K 4 3	♡ Q 9	♡ J 7
◇ A 4 2	◇ K 10 9 8 7	◇ A K Q 7 6 4 3
♣ J 5 3 2	♣ K 10 3	♣ 7 4 3

With *Hand E* bid 2NT. Just because it's 12 points, it doesn't make it a good hand. A 2NT response after a 1NT opening promises 11-12 points, and you are not worth a penny more.

With *Hand F* bid 3NT. With the five-card suit and the tens, this hand is worth about 13 points, and well worth the raise to game.

You should also bid 3NT on *Hand G*. Anyone who doesn't already respond 3NT quickly with this hand will improve their game overnight just by noting this example. Ten high-card points, plus three for the extra length in diamonds, makes it worth 13 points. However, what about *Hand H*?

Hand H	*Hand I*
♠ A K Q J 10 9	♠ 6 5 3
♡ 9 8	♡ A K Q 4
◇ J 8	◇ Q 9 6
♣ 7 6 2	♣ Q J 8

In simple Acol, I suppose that with *Hand H* you must bid 4♠ (or some ghastly misuse of Stayman to produce an invitational effect). Playing transfers, perhaps, you can invite game with a 3♠ rebid. But, even if you can make these bids, do you really want to? All too often one edges into a thin 4♠ contract, pleased at the science at one's disposal, only to find that partner holds *Hand I*. I have this sneaking feeling that the opponents may be defeating 4♠ on the combined hands, whilst 3NT looks to have decidedly good chances.

This is no set-up. This is an everyday occurrence, yet we spend more time staring longingly at that major suit. Especially when your suit is solid, it is much better to think of all long suits as equal assets for a no-trump contract, regardless of their denomination. Such bids are chancy, but the gains outweigh the risk.

Rubber bridge players will have the honours to consider. Perhaps it's a closer call now, but I'm still bidding 3NT.

Finally, a chance to turn the tables on aggressive opposition at match-pointed pairs. With more and more players doubling 1NT on a balanced 15 points, even 14, it is time to show that they have picked the wrong pair to try it on with.

You are West, holding *Hand J*, and the auction runs thus:

Hand J

♠ A 8			
♡ Q 3 2	**South**	**West**	**North**	**East**
◇ K 9 8		1NT	Dbl	NB
♣ K J 8 5 3	NB	?		

It is tempting to rescue yourself into 2♣ immediately, but the auction deserves a little more analysis.

The key bid is your partner's pass over North's penalty double. If partner had been very weak, say 0-3 points, he should have stuck in a bid straight away to muddy the waters. His pass tells you that he doesn't feel there is a better spot than 1NT, even doubled. This view marks him with about 4-9 points (I trust that he can redouble with 10+ points in your system, and that you are playing some kind of 'wriggle' to get out of 1NT doubled if necessary).

If partner is at the lower end of the 4-9 points scale, you will probably prefer to play in 2♣, whilst if he is maximum, 1NT doubled seems a good shot, particularly at Pairs. But let's go one further. What about 1NT redoubled? If the opponents don't chicken out — and one of them may well — you'll be putting yourself in for an outright top if you make the contract. If partner holds 7-9 points, I reckon you have a better than 50% chance of seven tricks, so it looks like a good bet.

So, to combine all your chances, this is what you do: you open 1NT, and it is doubled. If you, the opener, redouble, you are saying that you have a five-card suit which you would like to bid, but you are consulting your partner first. If partner fancies 1NT redoubled, he passes. If he is minimum and wants you to bid your suit, he relays with 2♣, and you either pass or correct to your suit.

This is a simple little bid to remember, and it is really quite powerful.

Go get 'em!

OUT OF TURN

A Tournament Director was called to a Mixed Table for a lead out of turn. The TD began to read out the long list of options, but the male player with the choice interrupted: 'Don't bother,' he said, 'to read out the one where partner gets to play the hand!'

From the IBPA Bulletin

SUCCESSFUL SACRIFICING

BY SU BURN

At a recent training weekend the hopefuls for the British Junior Teams were told one top player's views on slam-level sacrifices: there are only two types worth taking — those which cost less than the value of game and those which make.

Here are two examples from my own recent experience. The first cropped up in one of the matches in the British Bridge League's Premier League for teams of four:

Dealer: South
N/S Vul.

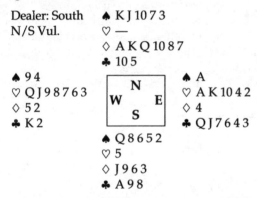

```
                    ♠ K J 10 7 3
                    ♡ —
                    ◊ A K Q 10 8 7
                    ♣ 10 5
  ♠ 9 4                              ♠ A
  ♡ Q J 9 8 7 6 3       N           ♡ A K 10 4 2
  ◊ 5 2            W         E      ◊ 4
  ♣ K 2                 S           ♣ Q J 7 6 4 3
                    ♠ Q 8 6 5 2
                    ♡ 5
                    ◊ J 9 6 3
                    ♣ A 9 8
```

At most tables South passed and West opened 3♡. North bid 4♡, showing a two-suiter, and East jumped to 6♡. South bid 6♠ which was passed round to East. The majority chose to take out insurance by bidding 7♡, as this contract looked unlikely to go more than three off — less than the value of game.

An exception was Alan Mould, my team-mate holding the East cards, who believes that his partner, Howard Melbourne, is one of the best opening-leaders in the game. He trusted Melbourne to find the killing lead (though why there should be one, I'm not certain) and passed 6♠ out.

Melbourne, true to form, led the ♣2, and 6♠ went one off for a 12-IMP gain.

The second hand came from a London Home Counties match:

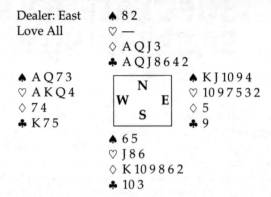

Dealer: East
Love All

North
♠ 8 2
♡ —
♢ A Q J 3
♣ A Q J 8 6 4 2

West
♠ A Q 7 3
♡ A K Q 4
♢ 7 4
♣ K 7 5

East
♠ K J 10 9 4
♡ 10 9 7 5 3 2
♢ 5
♣ 9

South
♠ 6 5
♡ J 8 6
♢ K 10 9 8 6 2
♣ 10 3

East passed and South, my partner, opened 2◇ showing a Weak Two in diamonds. West doubled for take-out and I jumped to 5◇. East bid 5♡ which was raised to 6♡ by West.

Feeling that 7◇ was unlikely to go more than two off, I took the sacrifice and West doubled.

However, West chose the unsuccessful lead of the ♡K, so the doubled grand slam made for +1630. At teams-of-eight scoring, this represented a 19-IMP gain.

No wonder our Juniors are performing so well, with such good advice!

EAVESDROPPINGS

Play at their table having ended, North-South sat and waited for forty-five minutes before their team-mates emerged from the other room.

'I've blown the match,' announced West, shaking his head disconsolately. 'I went down on the last board. I played it too quickly!'

Steve Johnston

MANIPULATE YOUR SMALL CARDS

BY BARRY RIGAL

When declarer, the play of the twos and threes may be as useful as the aces and kings. Your main scope for deception is the manipulation of small cards.

Declarer is in the position of being able to mislead both opponents without having to worry about confusing his partner. It does not matter if dummy gets the wrong count in a suit. Particularly at trick one, declarer can persuade either defender to continue a suit which is helpful to him by manipulating small cards.

A typical situation is illustrated by the hand below:

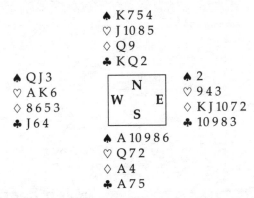

```
              ♠ K 7 5 4
              ♡ J 10 8 5
              ◇ Q 9
              ♣ K Q 2
 ♠ Q J 3            N            ♠ 2
 ♡ A K 6      W          E       ♡ 9 4 3
 ◇ 8 6 5 3         S            ◇ K J 10 7 2
 ♣ J 6 4                         ♣ 10 9 8 3
              ♠ A 10 9 8 6
              ♡ Q 7 2
              ◇ A 4
              ♣ A 7 5
```

South opens 1♠ and is raised to 4♠ by North. When West leads the ♡K, unless South conceals the ♡2 it will be easy for West to find the diamond switch at trick two. If South conceals the ♡2, West may well continue the suit hoping that partner holds ♡Q-3-2 or ♡3-2.

Once West continues with a second heart, the diamond loser can go away.

MAKE LIFE EASY ... FOR PARTNER

BY LES STEEL

My tip is a simple one on playing your cards in defence so as to make life easy for partner. For example, suppose partner leads the king of a suit in which you hold 9-7-3. You play the 3 (or the 9, if you use reverse count signals). If partner continues with the ace, your next card should show suit preference.

Here is a hand to illustrate the theme. The opponents bid:

South	North
1♠	2♠
4♠	End

You lead a club from the hand below, and this is what you see:

Dummy
♠ J 10 5 4
♡ 10 6 2
◇ 10 6 2
♣ A 4 3

You
♠ K 7
♡ A Q 7 3
◇ K 7 4
♣ 8 6 5 2

```
      N
   W     E
      S
```

Trick one goes small, ace, small, queen, and then declarer runs the ♠J to your king. You lead a second club which goes to small, king, and declarer's ruff. All follow to a trump to dummy's ♠10, then the ◇10 is run to your ◇K.

It is decision time! But if you exit passively waiting to make two heart tricks, you will be waiting for a long time, for declarer will be able to discard two of dummy's hearts on his long diamonds, as can be seen from the full deal *(diagram on next page)*.

How should you have known to play a heart? Look carefully at the full layout.

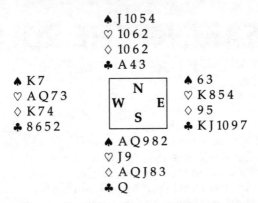

```
                    ♠ J 10 5 4
                    ♡ 10 6 2
                    ◊ 10 6 2
                    ♣ A 4 3
    ♠ K 7              N           ♠ 6 3
    ♡ A Q 7 3      W     E         ♡ K 8 5 4
    ◊ K 7 4           S            ◊ 9 5
    ♣ 8 6 5 2                      ♣ K J 10 9 7
                    ♠ A Q 9 8 2
                    ♡ J 9
                    ◊ A Q J 8 3
                    ♣ Q
```

The key was to notice partner's thoughtful ♣K at trick three. He had a choice of four cards to play from — the king, jack, ten and nine — so he must be screaming at you to play a heart. He was trying to do what all good partners should do: make things easy for you.

These situations are very common and can range from a subtle message to mild preference to a virtual command. So remember, since he or she is only human … *Try to make life easy for partner!*

DOUBLE TROUBLE

West opened 1♡, North doubled, and everybody passed. 'Don't you know that my double means "bid your longest suit", even if it is four cards to the six?' asked North.

'But I haven't got a four-card suit,' replied South, a beginner.

And, sure enough, the thirteenth card was on the floor under the table!

Mike Liver

BREAKING THE RULES

BY GUY DUPONT

Our most estimable bridge teachers try very hard to impress upon us a set of rules which — they say — enables us to be successful: cover an honour with an honour, second hand plays low, third hand high, don't lead into a tenace, etc.

Don't believe them! The only real rule in bridge is that there are no rules. Consider this hand, for example, played in a match between England and France for the *Entente Cordiale* Trophy:

```
Dealer: East        ♠ 6 5
Love All            ♡ A J 10 8 5 2
                    ◇ A J 2
                    ♣ 6 3
                              ♠ 9 8 7
                      N       ♡ Q 9 4
                  W       E   ◇ K Q 7 6 3
                      S       ♣ K 4
```

Closed Room:

South	West	North	East
Reardon	*Cronier*	*Butland*	*Lebel*
			NB
1♠	NB	2♡	NB
3♣	NB	3◇	NB
3♡	NB	4◇	NB
4NT	NB	5♡	NB
6♠	End		

Take Michel Lebel's place, defending from the East seat. West leads the ◇4 to dummy's ◇2 and your ◇Q. What do you play at trick two?

The bidding suggests that South has the ♡K doubleton. If declarer, as seems likely, has solid trumps, this is what will happen if you return a passive lead: declarer will draw trumps, and then he will play the ♡K, ♡A, and ruff a heart. The ◇A will then provide an entry to the established hearts in dummy.

144

This is why Lebel decided to *lead into the tenace* of dummy's ◇ A-J at trick two! Giving declarer a trick in order to deprive him of three was the killing defence, as can be seen from the full deal:

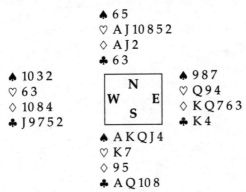

```
                    ♠ 6 5
                    ♡ A J 10 8 5 2
                    ◇ A J 2
                    ♣ 6 3
    ♠ 10 3 2          N          ♠ 9 8 7
    ♡ 6 3        W        E      ♡ Q 9 4
    ◇ 10 8 4         S          ◇ K Q 7 6 3
    ♣ J 9 7 5 2                  ♣ K 4
                    ♠ A K Q J 4
                    ♡ K 7
                    ◇ 9 5
                    ♣ A Q 10 8
```

Declarer was left with no alternative line: if he tried to ruff a club, he would be overruffed.

In the other room, Soulet-Reiplinger, playing against the Tredinnick twins, reached 3NT by South, a sensible contract. Too sensible — as, in practice, 6♡ will make more often than not, even on the ◇K lead. Declarer will test hearts by playing king and ace. The queen will not drop, but declarer retains control of the hand by playing four rounds of spades and discarding two diamonds; this line works if spades break 3-3, or even 4-2 if the long spades are held by the defender with the last trump.

The moral, in this case, is a defensive tip: *don't be afraid to lead into a tenace!**

Translated from the French by Elena Jeronimidis.

BRIDGE
A-BRAC

Yes, quite — you've had enough of the previous section and all the sound advice it contains. After all, I hear you say, bridge is not just about learning, it's about people, and fun, and getting it right! If that's the mood you're in, then this next section is just right for you: for it gives you a chance to test your skill as well as to read about the dreams, interests and follies of fellow bridge-players.

THE FAT-FINGERED LIZARD IS A FOE TO FEAR

BY KEN ROWE

As laughter breaks out at a table, the Club Director growls: 'Quiet! You've not come here to enjoy yourselves. You're here to play bridge.' But however serious the competition, or however badly you are doing, there is fun to be had playing bridge — by savouring the strange opponents who come your way.

I once read of a funeral director with a secret preoccupation. Whenever he met someone, he would imagine what they would look like in a coffin. He would size up the new acquaintance and be heard muttering: 'She would look lovely, so cool and restful,' or 'We could never make him look peaceful.'

Now I am not suggesting you should think of your opponents as corpses, though they can certainly look morbid as they coldly watch dummy go down. It's more intriguing to think of them as creatures bright and beautiful — as the late Victor Mollo did when he wrote about bridge in the menagerie.

You should explore the zoo. Have you met the Fat-fingered Lizard? He sits absolutely still, a predatory reptile. Only his hooded eyes move from hand to table. Suddenly he acts and you half expect a long tongue to flick out and strike a victim.

You may have met the Lesser Dormouse, a timid species, so meek her voice is rarely heard. A silent bidder is her ideal. While you are not looking, she can surreptitiously point to her bid — with an eraser on the end of her pencil to muffle the tap. 'Sorry, sorry' she mutters after some real or imagined mistake.

Of course, there's Mr Toad. His new enthusiasm is ignoring the opponents' system card. 'Don't need to know what you're up to, dear boy. I just bid my own hand, and blast away.' If aggression were the only quality needed, he would be totting up the Master Points. When he calls the Director, he makes it sound as if he is summoning the grand executioner.

Eeyore doesn't quite know what is going on. Or at least that's the impression he gives as he keeps turning the last card to see if it's red or black. Fumbled play is interspersed with: 'What contract am I in?' He never comes top, but he is never bottom either. That's because opponents overbid and scramble over themselves to double his contracts. And all the time he has so many points even he cannot fail to get his tricks.

Then there's Bear. No, not Pooh, nor Rupert, nor Paddington. This is a She-bear with a very sore head indeed. As you sit down, your convention card is snatched away and studied as if it contained the secret of everlasting life. Her own card is so complicated it would take a code-breaker to decipher it. She knows the rules like a barrack-room lawyer, but clearly she has not reached the proprieties, Part VII, section III: 'A player ... should carefully avoid any remark or action that might cause annoyance or embarrassment.'

Perhaps Owl is the most intimidating of all. You're left in no doubt that he knows more than you do — about everything. He has identified every card in your hand, and gives the impression he knows which mistake you're going to make next.

Sometimes he is partnered by Tawny Owl. They speak only to one another, ignoring you, while they pick over the entrails of the previous hand.

A bird of a different feather is Jemima Puddleduck (who, as you'll remember, always laid her eggs in the wrong place, just where sly old fox would find them). At the bridge table, Mrs Puddleduck hesitates, hovering over every suit in her hand. At last she selects a card — only to put it back again. Finally she plays with a sigh that indicates she knows that partner will not be pleased.

The catalogue of characters is endless. Watch out for Weasel, Hare and Tortoise; for Squirrel Nutkin, who hoards his trumps; for Boa Constrictor, that specialist in the squeeze. You may even come across the partner of my dreams: a rare species, clever as a fox in the bidding, sprightly as a gazelle in the play, the memory of an elephant, and the composure of a beautiful white dove.

With all this wildlife to study it is sometimes difficult to concentrate on the game. What did the lead of the ◊6 mean? What was that early discard by East? Meanwhile, a Black Mamba on my right is poised to strike ...

1ST JANUARY QUIZ

BY MIKE LAWRENCE

West leads the ♠K and ♠A against 4♡. East follows with the ♠10 and then signals with the ♣9.

Dealer: South	♠ J 5
E/W Vul.	♡ A
	◇ A K Q 9 3
	♣ K 10 7 5 4

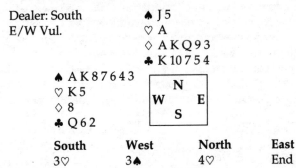

♠ A K 8 7 6 4 3
♡ K 5
◇ 8
♣ Q 6 2

South	West	North	East
3♡	3♠	4♡	End

East seems to have the ♣A, so getting a club trick and a heart later will set 4♡. What should West do at trick three?

(Solution on page 174)

CAKES & CONVENTIONS

BY ULRICH AUHAGEN

At the start of the next round, my partner informed me that our opponents played the *Flannery* convention. 'Does your 2◊,' I asked, 'show four spades and five hearts?' 'Not quite, because we play the Multi 2◊ and use 2♡ as Modified Flannery.'

Their convention card explained that 2♡ showed four spades, five hearts, no void, and 11-15 points. Over responder's 2NT relay asking opener to describe his hand further, the responses were:

3♣	= 4-5-1-3
3◊	= 4-5-3-1
3♡/3♠/3NT	= 4-5-2-2 (minimum/medium/maximum range of points)

I did my best to look impressed. 'In this way, we don't lose the Multi, so we can have our cake and eat it too!' Enjoying himself, right-hand opponent added, 'To test slam possibilities, responder at his next turn asks with 4♣ for controls, and opener responds step-wise, 0-2, 3, 4, and so on.' When I remained silent in admiration, he scribbled down:

Responder		*Opener (a)*	*Opener (b)*
♠ K x		♠ A Q x x	♠ A Q x x
♡ K x	N	♡ A x x x x	♡ A 10 x x x
◊ A K Q x x x	W E	◊ J x x	◊ x x
♣ Q 9 x	S	♣ x	♣ J x

'After partner's 2♡ opening,' West explained, 'if he holds *Hand A* we will reach the cold slam with *Auction A*, whereas on *Hand B* we'll stop in game with *Auction B*.'

Auction A		Auction B	
West	**East**	**West**	**East**
	2♡		2♡
2NT	3◊	2NT	3♡
4♣	4♠	3NT	End
6◊	End		

'We have to hurry up, I'm afraid,' our other opponent said. Partner and I smiled gratefully. With East the dealer and North-South vulnerable, these were my cards as North:

♠ A 10 8 5 4 2
♡ —
◇ A 8 5 3
♣ K 6 4

East on my left opened with 2♡, greeted with hilarity from us. Partner passed and West, the Master of Modified Flannery, relayed with 2NT.

On my left now 3♣ (4-5-1-3), and partner suddenly came to life with a double! When the Master on my right bid 3♡, non-forcing, in this awkward position I tried 4♡. East passed, 5♣ from partner, pass from West — and I, in a true Oscar-Wildeish mood (he could resist anything but temptation) — raised to 6♣. The complete auction thus was:

South	West	North	East
			2♡
NB	2NT	NB	3♣
Dbl	3♡	4♡	NB
5♣	NB	6♣	End

The ♡Q was led. When I tabled my hand, a worried partner eventually smiled and made his way to twelve tricks and 1370 to us. Master West regretted not having bid 4♡ immediately to silence everybody: 'I hoped to buy the contract cheaply,' he explained. 'You can't always have your cake and eat it,' I responded softly.

♠ A 10 8 5 4 2
♡ —
◇ A 8 5 3
♣ K 6 4

♠ 6
♡ 10 7 5 2
◇ K J 2
♣ A Q J 5 2

By the way, partner had to deal with this layout. Can you see the best line in 6♣ after a heart lead? *(Solution on next page)*

If you make use of the information provided by the bidding, the slam is cold.

Dummy ruffs the ♡Q lead and plays a small spade!

If East takes the trick to play his singleton diamond, declarer rises with the ◇K, ruffs a heart, ruffs a spade small, plays a trump to ♣K, and takes another spade ruff high.

A trump from East at trick three makes no difference: dummy takes the trick, then a spade ruff with a small trump, a heart ruff and another spade ruff lead to the same position.

Now declarer draws trumps, discarding diamonds, and dummy will take the last four tricks with the ◇A and the established spades. The full deal was:

Dealer: East
N/S Vul.

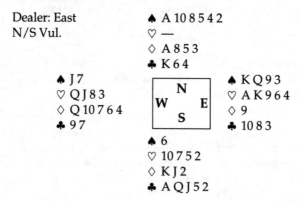

	♠ A 10 8 5 4 2	
	♡ —	
	◇ A 8 5 3	
	♣ K 6 4	
♠ J 7		♠ K Q 9 3
♡ Q J 8 3		♡ A K 9 6 4
◇ Q 10 7 6 4		◇ 9
♣ 9 7		♣ 10 8 3
	♠ 6	
	♡ 10 7 5 2	
	◇ K J 2	
	♣ A Q J 5 2	

BRITISH IS BEST

Playing at a club with silent bidders, rather than dabbing a pen to point at my bids I was using a small Spanish coin. After about sixteen boards, when my coin landed on the 'No Bid' square time after time, my partner handed me a £1 coin — it worked! The fact that I finally had something to say must prove that British is best.

Dodo Harley

A REAL TEST

BY TERENCE REESE AND NIKOS SARANTAKOS

This problem is from actual play at a high level. With East-West vulnerable and East the dealer, you are South, holding:

♠ K J 10 9 5
♡ J
◇ 8 2
♣ A Q J 4 2

East, opens 1♡, and you overcall 1♠ in preference to a Michaels 2♡. (In general, when you can overcall in spades on a two-suiter, this is better than the alternative.)

West bids 4♡, and your partner comes in with 4♠. The excitement is not over, for the bidding continues:

South	West	North	East
			1♡
1♠	4♡	4♠	5◇
NB	5♡	NB	NB
5♠	6♡	NB	NB
?			

This is very annoying. Are you going to pass, double, or bid on?

(Solution on page 164)

SLEEPLESS NIGHT

BY RICHARD BIRD

One of the best bridge books ever written is *Bridge with the Blue Team** by Pietro Forquet. I keep my copy on the bedside table and often read a page or two before drifting off, usually in a state of relaxed admiration. However, the other night I read about the following hand, describing a brilliant defence by Chiaradia in the 1958 European Teams Championship:

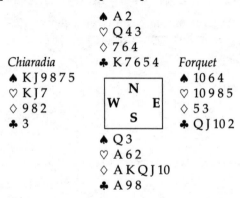

                          ♠ A 2
                          ♡ Q 4 3
                          ♦ 7 6 4
    Chiaradia   ♣ K 7 6 5 4   *Forquet*
    ♠ K J 9 8 7 5   ♠ 10 6 4
    ♡ K J 7   ┌─────────┐   ♡ 10 9 8 5
    ♦ 9 8 2   W │   N   │ E   ♦ 5 3
    ♣ 3   │   S   │   ♣ Q J 10 2
                        └─────────┘
                          ♠ Q 3
                          ♡ A 6 2
                          ♦ A K Q J 10
                          ♣ A 9 8

After a spade overcall by West, South played in 5♦. The lead was the ♣3 to the ♣10 and ♣A. South drew trumps, East discarding a low heart on the third round, and then led a low heart, expecting West to win and return the suit (South knows West has both the missing kings for his overcall). This way, a second entry to dummy is established, enabling declarer to duck a club and then set up the fifth one.

However, Chiaradia, West, foresaw this plan and played the ♡J on the ♡2, forcing South to use the ♡Q prematurely. Furthermore, when declarer came to hand with a heart to the ace, Chiaradia pitched the king. If he had not done so, he could have been thrown

---

*Bridge with the Blue Team by Pietro Forquet is published in the UK by Gollancz/Peter Crawley in the Master Bridge Series.

in to lead a spade. Forquet writes: 'At this stage the contract had become unmakeable. South tested the clubs, but was forced to surrender after the spade return.'

Duly impressed with this sublime defence, I put the book down and tried to sleep. But then a thought occurred to me: if declarer had played out the remaining trumps, wouldn't East be forced to come down to ♠10, ♡10, ◊ —, and ♣Q-J-2? Yes, he couldn't afford to throw a club, and with dummy keeping two spades and three clubs, he had to keep the ♡10 to protect West from being thrown in. Now South can endplay East by leading to the ♠A and exiting with a low club. East can cash the ♡10, but has to concede the last two clubs to dummy. Alternatively, South can exit with a heart, win the spade return in dummy, and again play a low club.

Ah, but no — that wouldn't work: at the end dummy has ♣K-7 and declarer ♠Q and ♣9. East can play a low club back and, owing to that infuriating blockage in clubs, the last trick has to be conceded to the defence. If only one of South's clubs had been interchanged with one of North's.

What about dummy retaining ♠A, ♡4, ◊ —, and ♣K-7-6 instead? If East comes down to the same cards as before, a spade to the ace and a heart exit will certainly endplay him this time. He would be forced to return a high club to dummy's king, and eventually allow the ♣7 to score.

Again, no: East, who was Forquet, would surely have risen to the occasion and thrown the ♡10, keeping two spades. That way, the heart guard that West had so courageously transferred to East would be handed back, killing declarer's chances. If only the ♡7 and ♡6 had been interchanged, the brilliance of both defenders might have been matched by that of the declarer.

What if South had played low to the ♡Q before drawing the third trump? What if South ducks the ♡J? What if South plays out all the trumps before touching hearts?

So many possibilities to analyse — so many sleepless hours to think about them.

AN INDIVIDUAL FOR NINE PLAYERS

BY GEOFF FOGG

Although hosts usually invite people so that they have eight, twelve or sixteen for their bridge parties, it is not always possible to get precisely these numbers. This is not a great cause for concern, as you can have a perfectly enjoyable bridge evening with only nine or ten players.

The following movement for nine players may be a useful example. Its main features are that nine rounds of three boards each are played, and that each person plays one round with each other player and at most three times against any other. As each player sits out once, the host may like to be Player 1 so as to be free to see to last-minute dinner arrangements in-between Rounds 5 and 6. The players are named A, B, C, D and 1, 2, 3, 4, the ninth contestant being R. Score as teams or match-pointed pairs.

COMPLETE INDIVIDUAL FOR 9 PLAYERS			
Round	TABLE 1	TABLE 2	Board
1	N/S A & B E/W C & D	N/S 1 & 2 E/W 3 & 4	1-3
2	N/S A & C E/W 1 & 3	N/S B & D E/W 2 & R	4-6
3	N/S A & 1 E/W B & 2	N/S D & 4 E/W C & R	7-9
4	N/S A & R E/W C & 4	N/S D & 3 E/W B & 1	10-12
5	N/S A & 4 E/W B & 3	N/S C & 2 E/W D & R	13-15
6	N/S A & D E/W 2 & 3	N/S B & R E/W 1 & 4	16-18
7	N/S A & 3 E/W 4 & R	N/S C & 1 E/W D & 2	19-21
8	N/S B & C E/W 2 & 4	N/S D & 1 E/W 3 & R	22-24
9	N/S A & 2 E/W 1 & R	N/S B & 4 E/W C & 3	25-27

TEST YOUR DEFENCE

BY BERNARD MAGEE

Defensive play is the most difficult aspect of bridge. The language used here is much less clear than that used in the auction. Every signal or non-signal seems to have any number of messages.

The most difficult part is trying to work as a team — so often one half of the partnership thinks of one line of defence, while the other finds a completely contrary and incompatible line. Whenever you think you have found a winning line, try to tell your partner — and furthermore, try to make the signal as clear as possible.

Teams-of-four	Dummy		
Dealer: South	♠ 9 2		
Game All	♡ K Q 7 4		
	◊ 8 7 6		
	♣ A K 6 2	You (Hand A)	You (Hand B)
		♠ J 6 5	♠ Q J 6
		♡ A J 5 3	♡ J 8 5 3
		◊ 5 2	◊ 5 2
		♣ 8 5 4 3	♣ Q 5 4 3

South	West	North	East
1NT	NB	2♣	NB
2◊	NB	3NT	End

South's opening no-trump was weak (12-14) and after a Stayman enquiry North pushed on to game — no qualms about his stringy 12-count.

Partner (West) leads the ♠7 to your ♠J and declarer's ♠K. Declarer follows with ◊K, ◊Q, and ◊J. Your partner takes the third round.

What do you play from *Hand A*? And would you play differently from *Hand B*?

(Solutions on page 168)

THE DAY I ARRIVED

BY RALPH CHURNEY

When I was a young lad of seventeen, a teacher for whom I had the highest regard told me that one day I would 'arrive' in this world to make my mark. What did he mean, and how would I know that I had 'arrived'? In which field of endeavour would I receive this accolade — a Nobel Prize or a knighthood?

Despite using Walter Mitty as a role model, I had no illusions as to my academic capabilities. Essentially a practical person, I nevertheless had two passions — music and fine art — but I came to realise that I lacked the talent to become either a pianist or an artist. What recognition I gained was swiftly tempered with disappointments, but I didn't brood: I just gave up painting and played bridge.

Over the next few years, I acquired various skills at the game and, although not at the forefront of the national selectors' eyes, I had a fair share of wins in national events. My ambition to represent Britain was fulfilled when my team forced itself into consideration by winning the Gold Cup: as a consequence, we were asked to represent Great Britain in the Europa Cup. Was that it? Had I now 'arrived'? No, it just didn't seem right, somehow.

Playing in an international, however, was an experience I will not forget. Bulgaria, Italy, Germany, Monaco and ourselves played a round robin, and the country lying top of the league at the end of the week would go forward to the final in Denmark about six months later. Here the winners would join the other finalists from five other heats to play in the Final.

Screens are an advantage to established partnerships. They prevent you from seeing partner's miserable expression when you do something he does not like (a frequent occurrence, in my case). Similarly, partner cannot see you looking puzzled by his bids (also a frequent occurrence). We got on famously and, surprisingly, we did well. Although at the start we were ranked a little above Monaco, with one round to go we were in the lead with a real chance to win the event. It seemed as though all hinged on the result of that last match.

In a match we desperately wanted to win, we started disastrously. Germany were beating us 25-5 VPs at half time, and on the first board of the second half my partner and I had a disaster:

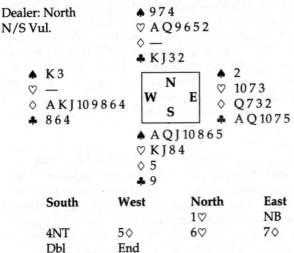

Dealer: North
N/S Vul.

♠ 974
♡ A Q 9 6 5 2
♢ —
♣ K J 3 2

♠ K 3
♡ —
♢ A K J 10 9 8 6 4
♣ 8 6 4

♠ 2
♡ 10 7 3
♢ Q 7 3 2
♣ A Q 10 7 5

♠ A Q J 10 8 6 5
♡ K J 8 4
♢ 5
♣ 9

South	West	North	East
		1♡	NB
4NT	5♢	6♡	7♢
Dbl	End		

Partner deals and opens 1♡ and I was looking at the South hand. I bid an uncultured 4NT Roman Blackwood, hoping it might stop any interference. It works like a damp squid at a bonfire. By the time it's my second turn to bid, we are at the seven level; I double East's 7♢, showing that I have a losing diamond.

I didn't realise I had thirteen losing cards. The opening lead was the ♡A and you can see what's coming. Declarer ruffed, drew trumps, played ♣4 to ♣10, and when I played the ♣9 he had no trouble figuring the situation. His losing spades went on the long clubs and 7♢ doubled made for 1440.

We knuckled down for a few hours and on the last board I picked up this hand as North and the following auction took place:

♠ 4 3
♡ A K 8
♢ Q J 6 4
♣ K Q 7 3

South	West	North	East
	1♠ (a)	Dbl	NB
2♢	2♠	3♢ (b)	3♠
NB	4♠	End	

(a) At least 5 spades, no more than 15 points.
(b) I am not sure this is the correct bid here.

Before reading on, you might care to choose your opening lead.

Just as I was beginning to give the matter proper consideration, we noticed that the board had been switched through 180°, which is why I was playing North instead of South. The Director ruled that play should continue, as no harm had been done.

I was deciding between my three natural leads of ♡A, ◇Q, and ♣K, when a warning bell rang in my ear. There was something not strictly kosher about the bidding. Why did East not bid 2♠ over my double? That would be the normal thing to do with three spades knowing that his partner held five. He only supported when we had bid and supported diamonds, and his partner had shown at least six spades. It appeared to me that he was prepared to let us play at a low level in clubs or hearts, but not diamonds. If my analysis of the situation was correct, the shape of his hand should then be 2-5-1-5 or 2-5-0-6 and, if so, dummy would be able to ruff diamonds.

I took a chance on looking a fool and led a trump. Partner won with the ♠A, returned a trump — and declarer gave me a look that could only be described as unfriendly. Not that I could blame him: as you can see from the full deal, any lead other than a trump gives the contract.

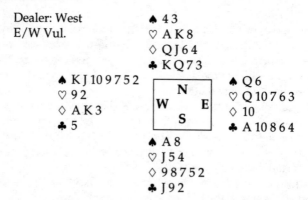

Dealer: West
E/W Vul.

North
♠ 4 3
♡ A K 8
◇ Q J 6 4
♣ K Q 7 3

West
♠ K J 10 9 7 5 2
♡ 9 2
◇ A K 3
♣ 5

East
♠ Q 6
♡ Q 10 7 6 3
◇ 10
♣ A 10 8 6 4

South
♠ A 8
♡ J 5 4
◇ 9 8 7 5 2
♣ J 9 2

'You would have found the same lead, wouldn't you?' I asked partner. 'Not in a million years,' was the succinct reply. He said this not to make me feel good, but as a rebuke, since he secretly thinks I have a guardian angel sitting on my right shoulder pulling random cards out of my left hand. I do not believe in guardian angels, but still it was strange that the board was switched at that particular moment so that I, with my crooked logic, would be placed on lead. Team-mates had a great set and, of course, made 4♠. Although we lost the match, we had won the round and had qualified for the Final — the first time a British team had done so.

Some months later, the team, loaded with instructions from well-wishers (in my case, mostly for LEGO from my youngsters) left for the Final in Copenhagen. On arrival, we were given VIP treatment and name-badges pinned to our lapels in case we forgot who we were, or tried to hide. The event was being held in a massive conference complex in Copenhagen, consisting of hotel rooms, theatre and function areas. Closed-circuit television would allow hundreds of people to watch the play in the Vu-Graph theatre which, to my amazement, turned out to be full every day from when play started to when it finished in the early hours of the morning.

On the afternoon of my first day in Copenhagen, I was walking across the lobby when a portly gentleman approached me, scrutinised my badge, came closer, and said: 'Are you ze Churney who led the ze four of spades in Italy?' Out of all the hands played, I knew exactly which one he meant. I grinned, and indicated that I was that person. 'Great lead, the hand is in both our national papers,' he continued, and showed me a copy of the Danish paper he was carrying. I did not understand a word of Danish, but I recognised the hand diagram. It was then I knew. It hit me, I had 'arrived.'

Unfortunately, having 'arrived,' I did not 'stay' for long. The following July, after being invited to play in Kenya, and being unsuccessful in defending the Gold Cup, I retired from serious competitive bridge for a while to enjoy some major surgery. But I will always remember that moment when I 'arrived'. I was 'ze Churney who led ze four of spades in Italy.'

I never dreamt, all those years ago when I envisaged at least a knighthood, that when I did 'arrive' it would be with a pack of cards — and in particular the four of spades!

A sad story, really.

A REAL TEST

PROBLEM BY REESE AND SARANTAKOS ON PAGE 155

This was Deal 63 of the final of the 1982 Rosenblum Cup Teams between France and the USA.

To sacrifice in 6♠ won't be very expensive — but who wants to go minus, when the opponents' action suggests they may have been pushed into an unmakeable slam? Other considerations are:

- Your partner may have been 'pushed' when he went to 4♠.

- East's 5♦ suggests that any diamond honour North may hold will be under the ace.

- Unless West has been playing a very deep game from the beginning, his hand seems to have improved. It is quite possible that he has length in spades and knows that his partner will be short.

- The ♣K is more likely to be on your left than on your right .

Enough of that. Chip Martel passed 6♡, and this was the full deal:

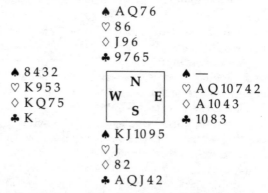

```
                    ♠ A Q 7 6
                    ♡ 8 6
                    ◇ J 9 6
                    ♣ 9 7 6 5
   ♠ 8 4 3 2                        ♠ —
   ♡ K 9 5 3          N             ♡ A Q 10 7 4 2
   ◇ K Q 7 5      W       E         ◇ A 10 4 3
   ♣ K                S             ♣ 10 8 3
                    ♠ K J 10 9 5
                    ♡ J
                    ◇ 8 2
                    ♣ A Q J 4 2
```

6♡ was lay-down, as you see. South cannot be blamed for passing. He did well not to double, which would have been 1660 instead of 1430. A point generally not appreciated is that at teams you gain little from doubling a borderline slam and lose quite heavily if it makes. At the other table the auction was more revealing and the sacrifice became obvious. 6♠ doubled was three down, for minus 500.

EXPERTS ARE HUMAN

BY DANNY ROTH

The following hand came up in a quiz programme run by two of our leading players some years ago:

♠ A 4 2
♡ 6 4
◇ K Q 10 7 5 3
♣ 4 3

♠ K J 6
♡ A Q 8 7
◇ A
♣ A K 10 7 5

Against silent opposition, South reaches 3NT and West leads the ♣2, East playing the ♣Q. Decide on your line of play before reading on. Is the contract guaranteed against any defence and distribution?

The first contestant, a man, recommended winning the first club and cashing the ◇ A. Now he crossed to the ♠A and tested the diamonds, discarding two low clubs. When they failed to split, he turned to hearts, leading low from dummy and just covering whatever East put on, hoping eventually to take a second heart trick in addition to the eight top winners outside.

The adjudicators judged this wrong, correctly pointing out that, if West has the diamond length, he will be in a position to cash the ◇J when in with the first round of hearts, assuming that East has played the ♡9, ♡10, or ♡J to the ♡Q and ♡K. Declarer's hand is now strip-squeezed. Whatever he discards, West will return that suit, and now declarer could be held to eight tricks.

The second contestant, a woman, assumed that the lead was fourth-highest and ducked the first round. She would win a club continuation and continue the suit. On the assumption of a 4-2 split, she would gain a third club trick to join six top winners outside.

The judges pronounced this the 'correct' solution.

Well, this is certainly one up for *Why Women Win at Bridge*! But, in my opinion, the 'experts' were wrong on two counts. What are they?

The contract is, in fact, a 100% certainty on the diamond line — the first contestant missed a small point. Consider the layout once again:

♠ A 4 2
♡ 6 4
◇ K Q 10 7 5 3
♣ 4 3

♠ K J 6
♡ A Q 8 7
◇ A
♣ A K 10 7 5

On the third round of diamonds, someone will show out, otherwise there is no problem. If West shows out (i.e. East has the diamond length), declarer can safely turn to hearts, just covering whatever East puts on.

Out of diamonds, West must return a heart (or concede a free black-suit finesse) and now declarer can establish a second heart trick by weight of cards. If East shows out (i.e. West has the diamond length), South simply plays a fourth round of diamonds, discarding the ♡7, and West is now endplayed, forced to give a free finesse in any non-diamond suit. Note that, even if diamonds are 5-1 or 6-0, this line still holds as South can spare the ♡8 on the fifth round of diamonds. The contract is assured.

As regards the line chosen by the second contestant, all will be well if the clubs are 4-2 but, if the lead turns out to be a deceptive one from a five-card suit and East switches to a spade at trick two (which would be a better defence even if the suit did break 4-2, since continuing clubs in the knowledge that declarer holds five would be self-defeating), South can no longer guarantee the contract. I leave it to the reader to prove this as an exercise.

Points to remember:

1. It will usually be correct to trust opponents' line of defence as reasonable and take it at face value — but why take unnecessary risks?

2. Be wary of assuming that top-class players are *always* right. Even experts are human — do not take whatever they say as gospel!

CAN YOU DO BETTER?

BY NIGEL GUTHRIE

Hands similar to those below occurred at teams events in Bournemouth and Stratford. The expert declarers failed in their contracts. Can you do better?

Hand 1
E/W Vul.

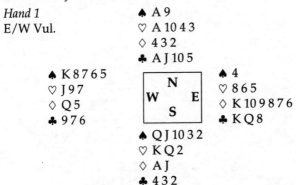

As South, plan the play in 4♠, doubled by West. In the course of the auction, East overcalled 2◇. West leads the ◇Q.

Hand 2
Love All

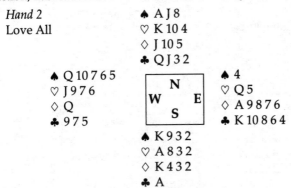

Plan the play as South, declarer in 3NT. The opposition has been silent throughout the auction. West leads the ♠6, and East follows with ♠4.

(Solutions on page 182)

TEST YOUR DEFENCE

PROBLEMS BY BERNARD MAGEE ON PAGE 159

Holding *Hand A* we want partner not to continue spades but to play a heart, enabling us to return a spade and defeat 3NT by one. Surely the ♡J is our clearest signal.

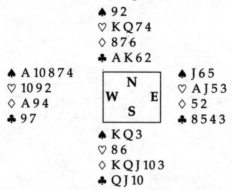

With *Hand B*, we want partner to continue spades. Here we do best to analyse the lead more closely: the ♠7. We have seen, or can see, the ♠K-Q-J-9; this leaves just ♠A-10-8 above the ♠7 — and in partner's hand! Our clearest signal must be the ♠Q.

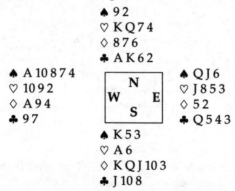

Try to think what signals will be clearest for partner to understand: this is the key to a good defensive team.

EETS

BY ALAN HIRON

The late Terence Reese and David Bird wrote an excellent book entitled *That Elusive Extra Trick* — an evocative title that brings two stories to mind ...

Quite recently, when I was playing in 3NT, a critical finesse failed and my opponents unsportingly ran a long suit. Gently my partner murmured, 'You must read my forthcoming book, *Those Elusive Five Extra Tricks.*'

I gave him a wintry smile but was reminded of a match against unknown opponents who played a complex relay system. An early board found them indulging in about ten rounds of incomprehensible bidding. When they finally ground to a halt — in 6◊, I think — we asked for some explanations. It appeared that dummy knew absolutely nothing about his partner's hand (he had merely answered questions) but declarer was able to describe the dummy that was due to appear in minute detail.

'I expect to find four spades headed by the ace, a doubleton heart, three diamonds to the jack, and two of the top three honours in clubs.' I led, and dummy duly appeared with:

♠ A 9 7 3
♡ 8 5
◊ J 7 2
♣ A Q 8 5

My heart sank — they really seemed to know what they were doing — and declarer thanked his partner with a beaming smile.

I need not have worried for, against perfectly normal breaks, there proved to be no fewer than three Elusive Extra Tricks (EETs). The operation was a success, but the patient died.

Well, you only need one EET on the deal shown overleaf:

Dealer: South
Love All

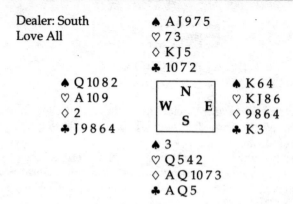

♠ A J 9 7 5
♡ 7 3
◇ K J 5
♣ 10 7 2

♠ Q 10 8 2
♡ A 10 9
◇ 2
♣ J 9 8 6 4

♠ K 6 4
♡ K J 8 6
◇ 9 8 6 4
♣ K 3

♠ 3
♡ Q 5 4 2
◇ A Q 10 7 3
♣ A Q 5

South opened 1◇ and North responded 1♠. With an awkward rebid, South chose 1NT (even though this purported to show 15-17 points) and an optimistic North raised to game. West led the ♣6 against 3NT, and at least declarer was off to a fair start when he won East's ♣K with his ♣A.

There were still only eight tricks in sight and no obvious chances for a ninth. Following the principle that when you run a long suit your opponents may run into real or imagined difficulties with their discards, South rattled off five rounds of diamonds. This left West with four discards to find, and he parted with three of his spades and the ♡9.

Next declarer cashed dummy's ♠A and led a low heart from the table. East and South played low, and West found himself fixed. If he won with ♡10, he could cash the ace but would then have to lead away from the ♣J. Desperately he won the first heart with the ace and exited with the ♡10; East won with his ♡K and could cash ♠K, but by now South's ♡Q had been set up as the EET.

It is worth noting that it was East who misdefended. When the heart was led from the table, he should have gone in with his king — a play that could hardly cost. When it wins, he can push a club through and his partner is out of all trouble.

My other EET hand proved an interesting affair featuring what can only be described as an 'involuntary *grand coup*' and an intriguing missed opportunity for the defence:

Dealer: South
Game All

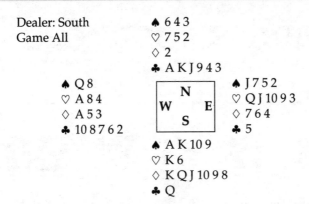

```
                      ♠ 6 4 3
                      ♡ 7 5 2
                      ◇ 2
                      ♣ A K J 9 4 3
    ♠ Q 8                             ♠ J 7 5 2
    ♡ A 8 4          N                ♡ Q J 10 9 3
    ◇ A 5 3      W       E            ◇ 7 6 4
    ♣ 10 8 7 6 2      S               ♣ 5
                      ♠ A K 10 9
                      ♡ K 6
                      ◇ K Q J 10 9 8
                      ♣ Q
```

Playing Precision Club, South opened 1♣ (16+ points) and North responded 2♣. South showed his diamonds, North repeated his clubs, and South tried 3♠. With little else to do, North bid clubs for a third time, and South made a well-judged club raise — the best game, with the right declarer!

West led the ♣2 against 5♣, and after winning South led the ◇Q. West won and, hoping for an eventual trump trick, played ace and another heart. Dummy had to be entered in order to draw trumps, so declarer was forced to ruff one of his winning diamonds — the so-called *grand coup*. Now a top trump revealed the position and, after coming to hand with a top spade, South ran his diamonds. Dummy's trumps, you will notice, had been reduced to the same length as West's and, when West ruffed, dummy could overruff and draw the remaining trumps. Then South, if necessary, could come back to hand with a spade to enjoy any remaining diamonds.

I mentioned a possibility for the defence: suppose that, instead of cashing the ♡A, West had led a spade with the idea of removing one of the two essential spade entries to South's hand? This might well ruin any attempt at the trump coup.

Ah! But which spade should West lead? The ♠Q exposes East's ♠J to a finesse, and South still has the two spade entries he needs. A really cunning West might try the ♠8. The jack loses to the king and, of course, South can still get home by dropping West's now lone ♠Q. Equally, though, he might well play for East to hold ♠Q-J, and so finesse — unsuccessfully — on the second round.

Would South have got it right? Alas, we shall never know …

BRIDGE CROSSWORD

BY NEIL WARD

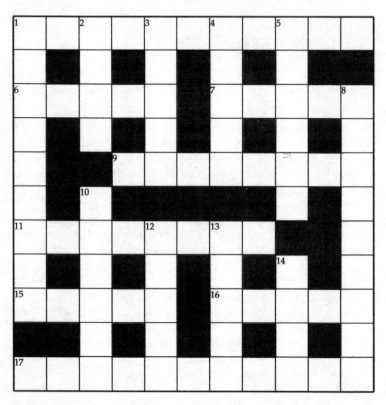

Across:

1. Pulls contract perhaps in, protection for keeps (11)
6, 14D Bird's nude swimming doesn't promise much (9)
7. Eccentrics presented by visitors at table? (5)
9. Bridge personality has day abroad and I worry (8)
11. Add up sum, one with opponents (8)
15. Wants partners to hold back letter (5)
16. Very hard pirate in bridge? (5)
17. He knows name is unusual (4, 7)

Down:

1. 7, a pair but good for Gooch! (9)
2. Betters score with cutting tool we hear (4)
3. Ass from Yarborough dancing hay; go away (5)
4. Suffer from strain curiously enough (5)
5. European composer? (6)
8. One heavyweight may be in hand (9)
10. Run out of clothes (6)
12. Fails and finishes headless (5)
13. O. Sharif spends hour making capital (5)
14. See 6 across

(Solution below)

1ST JANUARY SOLUTION

PROBLEM BY MICHAEL LAWRENCE ON PAGE 151

West should lead a heart. If you look at the diagram, you will see why.

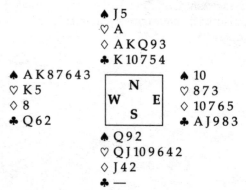

```
                    ♠ J 5
                    ♡ A
                    ◇ A K Q 9 3
                    ♣ K 10 7 5 4
    ♠ A K 8 7 6 4 3              ♠ 10
    ♡ K 5                        ♡ 8 7 3
    ◇ 8            W      E       ◇ 10 7 6 5
    ♣ Q 6 2          S           ♣ A J 9 8 3
                    ♠ Q 9 2
                    ♡ Q J 10 9 6 4 2
                    ◇ J 4 2
                    ♣ —
```

If West leads a club, South ruffs and then ruffs his ♠Q with dummy's ace. South can get back to his hand with another club ruff and will go about drawing trumps. West gets his ♡K, but that is the end of that.

Note that if West leads a diamond at trick three, South does the same thing, winning in hand and ruffing his spade.

Leading a third round of spades is also a tempting defence, but South just ruffs it with the ace and goes about the business of getting rid of the trumps.

By leading the heart at trick three, West is now able to get in with the ♡K and can give East a spade ruff. That annoying ♡A isn't in dummy any more to stop this.

BRIDGE MOVIE (WITH A MORAL)

BY PETER HAWKES

You are playing standard fourth-highest and top-of-sequence leads, and distributional signals and discards. After the auction below, your partner (West) leads the ♠10.

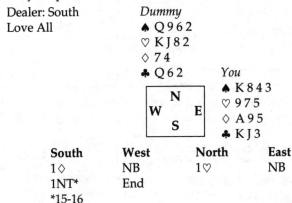

Dealer: South
Love All

Dummy
♠ Q 9 6 2
♡ K J 8 2
◊ 7 4
♣ Q 6 2

You
♠ K 8 4 3
♡ 9 7 5
◊ A 9 5
♣ K J 3

South	West	North	East
1◊	NB	1♡	NB
1NT*	End		
*15-16			

The first trick begins ♠10, ♠2, ♠4, and after some thought declarer takes it with the ♠A. Declarer cashes the ♡A (♡4, ♡2, ♡5) and the ♡Q (♡3, ♡8, ♡7), and then leads the ♣10 to partner's ♣4, dummy's ♣2, and your ♣J which takes the trick.

What can you say about the unseen hands?

In the face of bids in diamonds and hearts, partner appears to have chosen a short-suit lead of the ♠10 from ♠10-x doubleton; declarer therefore won the first trick with the ♠A from ♠A-J-x, preserving the ♠J-x to provide a sure entry to dummy. The entry problem was confirmed by declarer's subsequent cashing of the doubleton ♡A-Q. Partner's ♣4 was his lowest, indicating a three-card suit (since with five he probably would have led one), and declarer's ♣10 strongly suggests that he also holds the ♣9. Declarer began with 11 points in the major suits, and therefore 4 or 5 in the minor suits; this leaves 5 or 6 for partner, also in the minor suits.

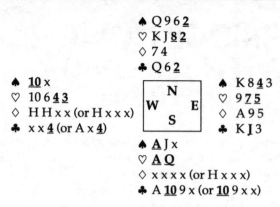

♠ Q962
♡ KJ82
◇ 74
♣ Q62

♠ 10 x
♡ 1064 3
◇ H H x x (or H x x x)
♣ x x 4 (or A x 4)

♠ K843
♡ 975
◇ A 95
♣ K J 3

♠ A J x
♡ A Q
◇ x x x x (or H x x x)
♣ A 10 9 x (or 10 9 x x)

*Can you see any hope of beating the contract,
and what do you lead at trick five?*

If declarer has the ♣A, then he has the potential to take two tricks in spades, four in hearts, and three in clubs. Before that, you could cash the ♠K and four diamond tricks (if partner is as good as ◇K-Q-8-x) to go with the ♣J already taken. The contract would make unless declarer makes a mistake.

So, assume that partner has the ♣A, and therefore that declarer has ◇K-J-x-x or ◇K-Q-x-x, and reconsider. You have a total of one spade trick, probably two diamond tricks, and three club tricks — not enough. Declarer has a total of two spade tricks, four heart tricks, and at least one trick in the minor suits — seemingly plenty of tricks — but they are not yet established and the lack of communication between the North and South hands will cause problems. A club lead now from you would make things easy for declarer (especially if he does have the ♣A after all). You could try the ♠3 or the ♡9, forcing declarer to choose discards from his own hand before he is ready, but this makes no progress towards establishing tricks for the defence.

Let's say that you lead the ◇5 to declarer's ◇J, partner's ◇Q, and dummy's ◇4. A second round of diamonds would be the best continuation but, perhaps reading you for better spades, partner returns the ♠7, covered by dummy's ♠9.

Pause to reconstruct the hand at this stage.

You still don't know whether partner's remaining high card is the ♣A or the ◇K, but continue to assume the former since that will be necessary for a successful defence.

176

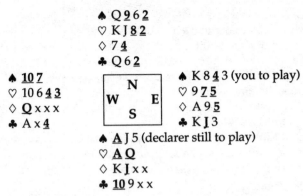

Do you take the ♠K and, if so, how do you continue?

Holding up will not work: declarer will cash his remaining heart winners, and then lead up to his ◇K (or ♣A). So you take the ♠K, declarer following (after some thought) with the ♠5.

Declarer will succeed if you exit with a heart, or if you play ace and another diamond; and cashing clubs only delays the problem. But look at the effect of the ♠3: declarer cannot afford to overtake his own ♠J with dummy's ♠Q, since that would establish the setting trick with your ♠8.

Trick seven therefore consists of the ♠3, ♠J, ♡6, and ♠6. Declarer gets off lead with a club, and your side takes the ♣A and ♣K at tricks eight and nine. You exit with ace and another diamond. Declarer wins the ◇K and cashes his long club, but partner is still there to take the last trick with the ◇10 for one off.

The full deal was:

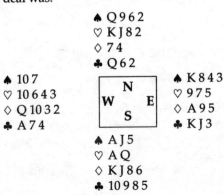

Could declarer have done any better? Yes, the ♠Q at trick one (which East must allow to hold) is a better start. The contract can then be made if South makes the odd-looking play of a club at trick two, or if he guesses to rise with the ◊K on the first round of the suit. Would declarer have done better to have unblocked the ♠J under the king at trick six? No, the defence can eliminate dummy's minor suits and then throw him in with a heart, to concede the final trick to East's ♠8.

At the table, the bidding and play proceeded as described in the article until trick seven when I carelessly played ace and another diamond, allowing declarer to score two spades, four hearts, and the ◊K.

The Moral(s)

1. Count the tricks available to the declarer and the defence as soon as you can. Even if declarer appears to have more than enough strength to make his contract, don't give up if he hasn't also got enough tricks.

2. Even when declarer appears to have enough tricks, he may not be able to establish and enjoy them if communications are difficult and suits are blocked. Watch the spot cards and don't give anything away.

EAVESDROPPINGS

West led ace and another spade against a 6♣ contract which everyone at the table could see was cold. Declarer won, and tackled trumps. With six clubs to the jack in dummy and five to the A-K in hand, she played the ♣A and noted West's discard of a spade. Several minutes later, she triumphantly played the ♣K, dropping the ♣Q.

'A nice piece of counting,' commented East drily.

BRIDGE MIRACLES

BY ERWIN SCHÖN

W hat are miracles? Can the impossible really happen, or is it only our limited knowledge that makes us perceive certain events as 'miraculous'?

This debate has been going on for a long time among philosophers and scientists, but bridge-players could well contribute to it, too.

Personally I maintain that in bridge the impossible can happen, though it is rare that an explanation to a seemingly impossible result cannot be found. Sometimes the explanation lies with the whims of fortune, but more often than not it is a human error or good, logical thinking that brings the 'miracle' about.

To illustrate this point, here are three well-known hands from the past. Do you remember *The Mississippi Gamblers' Hand*?

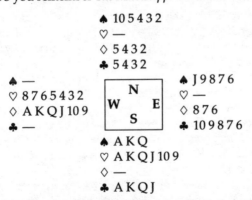

```
                    ♠ 10 5 4 3 2
                    ♡ —
                    ◇ 5 4 3 2
                    ♣ 5 4 3 2
   ♠ —                           ♠ J 9 8 7 6
   ♡ 8 7 6 5 4 3 2    N          ♡ —
   ◇ A K Q J 10 9   W   E        ◇ 8 7 6
   ♣ —                 S         ♣ 10 9 8 7 6
                    ♠ A K Q
                    ♡ A K Q J 10 9
                    ◇ —
                    ♣ A K Q J
```

Whatever game contract South might bid is doubled by West.

In the old days, a redoubled contract could be re-redoubled *ad infinitum*. The story says that Charles M. Schwab, the wealthy American stockbroker, paid out $10,000 on this hand!

My next hand occurred during the 1991 Fall National in Indianapolis in the Victory Swiss Team-of-four event, in the match between the favourites and an unfancied team:

Dealer: North
Love All

```
                    ♠ K Q 9 7 2
                    ♡ 8
                    ◇ 8
                    ♣ A Q J 9 7 3
  ♠ 6 4 3                              ♠ A J 10 8 5
  ♡ A J 7 5 3         N                ♡ 9 4
  ◇ K 7 6 4      W         E           ◇ A 5
  ♣ 5                 S                ♣ 10 8 6 4
                    ♠ —
                    ♡ K Q 10 6 2
                    ◇ Q J 10 9 3 2
                    ♣ K 2
```

South	West	North	East
		1♣	NB
1♡	NB	1♠	NB
2NT	NB	3♠	NB
3NT	NB	NB	Dbl
Redbl	End		

West's opening lead of the ♠6 was covered by dummy's ♠Q. East won, and continued with the ♠J, won in dummy with the ♠K. A heart was led to the king in the South hand, ducked by West, and then South led the ◇3 to dummy's ◇8. East was convinced that his partner had the ♣K and decided to duck. Curtains! Declarer (a member of the unfancied team) reeled off six club tricks and claimed the contract, for 800 to North-South.

Obviously West had not helped matters by ducking the ♡K — but then West, too, was certain that his partner held the ♣K!

In the other room, North played in 4♣ losing four tricks for a score of minus 50.

Of course, the contract should have been beaten. But all players occasionally make mistakes, and once they form the opinion that partner has a certain card (here the ♣K) it is easy to go wrong.

In the next hand, used in the bridge lessons of Eddie Kantar, declarer has to perform what may well look like a real miracle:

South	West	North	East
			3◇
6♠	End		

♠ 8 3
♡ J 10 7
◇ 10 8 6
♣ A K J 10 5

♠ A K Q J 7 6 5 2
♡ A K 3
◇ A 3
♣ —

Against 6♠, West leads the ◇2. Declarer wins and lays down the ♠A, East discarding the ◇4. It would appear that South has no entry to dummy to discard his losers; however, this is a mirage.

The diamond lead is obviously a singleton, therefore all declarer needs to do is play another top spade and then endplay West with the ♠2.

Whatever West leads, declarer's losers will vanish and the contract will be made, for the full deal is:

Dealer: East
Love All

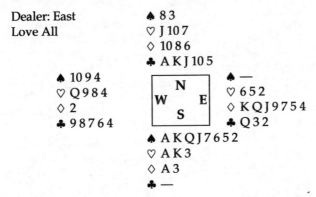

♠ 8 3
♡ J 10 7
◇ 10 8 6
♣ A K J 10 5

♠ 10 9 4
♡ Q 9 8 4
◇ 2
♣ 9 8 7 6 4

♠ —
♡ 6 5 2
◇ K Q J 9 7 5 4
♣ Q 3 2

♠ A K Q J 7 6 5 2
♡ A K 3
◇ A 3
♣ —

A miracle? Well, no — just plain logical thinking.

CAN YOU DO BETTER?

PROBLEMS BY NIGEL GUTHRIE ON PAGE 167

Hand 1

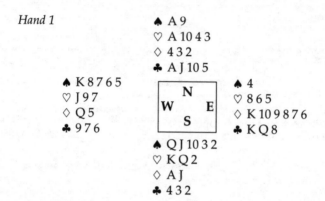

♠ A 9
♡ A 10 4 3
◇ 4 3 2
♣ A J 10 5

♠ K 8 7 6 5
♡ J 9 7
◇ Q 5
♣ 9 7 6

♠ 4
♡ 8 6 5
◇ K 10 9 8 7 6
♣ K Q 8

♠ Q J 10 3 2
♡ K Q 2
◇ A J
♣ 4 3 2

The only danger to your contract is if the defenders force you to ruff diamonds. To prevent this, duck the ◇Q. If West switches to clubs (best), finesse dummy's ten. Win the diamond return and play the ♠A-9. When West ducks, cross to the ♡Q and drive out the ♠K. Win West's club exit with the ♣A and cross to the ♡K to draw trumps.

Hand 2

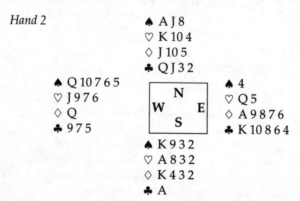

♠ A J 8
♡ K 10 4
◇ J 10 5
♣ Q J 3 2

♠ Q 10 7 6 5
♡ J 9 7 6
◇ Q
♣ 9 7 5

♠ 4
♡ Q 5
◇ A 9 8 7 6
♣ K 10 8 6 4

♠ K 9 3 2
♡ A 8 3 2
◇ K 4 3 2
♣ A

Your best chance to develop two diamond tricks is to lead twice towards the hand with two honours. Hence, you overtake dummy's ♠8 with your ♠9, and lead small towards ◇J-10.

182

SOLO BRIDGE

BY STEPHEN CASHMORE

❏ ELIMINATION & ENDPLAY	❏ BATH COUP
❏ AVOIDANCE	❏ BLOCKING
❏ DISCOVERY	❏ DUMMY REVERSAL

Iwas about to make a choice from the on-screen list when my cat Eric jumped up on the keyboard, strolled across it, and escaped out of the window. As a result, when the following hand flashed up, I had no idea how I was supposed to play it:

♠ 7 6
♡ 7 3 2
◇ A K 9 3 2
♣ K 9 7

Apparently I am in a contract of 2NT, played by South, and the computer-West has led the ♠4. If East plays the ♠Q, then I might consider whether I have to hold off the first trick, since my ♠K-J will then be equivalent to a holding like ♠A-x. But no, East plays the ♠10 and I win with my ♠J.

♠ K J 5
♡ A K 9
◇ 7 6 4
♣ A 6 4 2

What's going on here? Has the computer miscounted tricks? It looks as if I should win at least three tricks in the majors, two in clubs, and four in diamonds. So why am I only in 2NT? I look suspiciously at the diamonds. No doubt they are going to break 4-1 or even 5-0 and I have to find a way of getting round it.

Let's see. At trick two I play a small diamond towards dummy. West plays the ◇8. Briefly, I consider playing the ◇9 as some sort of safety play — but only briefly. If East wins and fires back a spade, West might be able to take five more which along with the diamond would see me one down. So I click on a top diamond.

Well, either the diamonds will break or they won't. I play the ◇K and — good news — both defenders follow. Then I play a third round to set up the suit and — bad news — East wins with the ◇J.

As I half expected, East plays back a spade and West has five left. One down. And I thought I was going to make an overtrick!

I count again, more carefully this time. One spade, two hearts, two clubs makes five. So I need only three diamonds. Maybe there is some safety play available, although SAFETY PLAY does not appear in the list of options to select. Ah, well, life doesn't generally give you a convenient list either.

Reset the deal. Win the first spade, then play a diamond to the ♢9. No good. East wins the jack again, and West cashes spades to defeat the contract.

Curses. Reset the deal again. How about not winning the first spade? I can't see how it will help, but the computer might switch the spades around for some reason to make it worthwhile. I duck the first spade and East continues with a second. West takes five more, so this time I am down even before touching the diamonds. Double curses!

OK, OK, calm down and let the computer have a go. I press the necessary keys and sit back to watch, perhaps to learn. Spade led, won with the jack. Diamond played to the ♢8 and ♢A. Good so far. Back to hand with a top heart and a second diamond led — OK, I didn't do that, but I don't see … oh! West has played the ♢Q and the computer-declarer promptly ducked in dummy!

Of course, it's all so obvious now. It is an AVOIDANCE PLAY. Declarer has to set up diamonds without letting East into the lead. If East has ♢Q-x-x, or ♢Q-J-x, or four diamonds, it cannot be done, but with any other diamond layout West can be forced to win a diamond trick early on. And West cannot harm the contract from that side of the table.

These avoidance plays can be hard to spot. Maybe I'll surprise partner, now that I've seen it done on screen, by spotting one in actual play.

184

DOUBLE DUMMY

BY RICHARD WHEEN

North is on lead in a heart contract. How are North-South to make all six tricks against any defence?

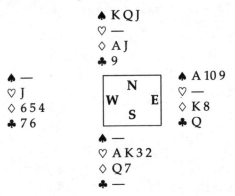

♠ K Q J
♡ —
◇ A J
♣ 9

♠ —
♡ J
◇ 6 5 4
♣ 7 6

N
W　E
S

♠ A 10 9
♡ —
◇ K 8
♣ Q

♠ —
♡ A K 3 2
◇ Q 7
♣ —

(Solution below)

SOLUTION TO DOUBLE DUMMY PROBLEM

North starts by leading a spade, which South ruffs high to prevent West from winning the trick. In view of South's need to ruff, East does best to play low on this trick. South now leads his other heart honour (removing West's trump) and another heart. On these leads North discards (in either order) a spade and ◇J. On the first of these East can safely discard a spade, but on the second he has to unguard one of three suits. If he throws a black card, he promotes North's card in that suit, so he will probably discard the ◇8 — in which case South leads his ◇7 to North's ◇A. North leads either of his remaining cards for South to ruff, and ◇Q is good for the last trick.

185

POST-MORTEM

BY SALLY BROCK

The match had finished, and my team sat down to discuss our scorecards.

'Sorry about Board 1,' I said. 'I suppose we got too high, but it is difficult to stop out of game.'

'Were you in 3NT or four spades?'

'Four spades, but I don't think it matters much.'

This was the deal we were talking about:

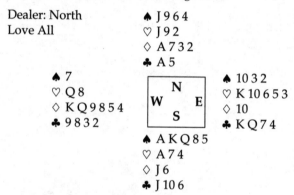

Dealer: North
Love All

North
♠ J 9 6 4
♡ J 9 2
◇ A 7 3 2
♣ A 5

West
♠ 7
♡ Q 8
◇ K Q 9 8 5 4
♣ 9 8 3 2

East
♠ 10 3 2
♡ K 10 6 5 3
◇ 10
♣ K Q 7 4

South
♠ A K Q 8 5
♡ A 7 4
◇ J 6
♣ J 10 6

My partner and I had had an uninterrupted auction:

South	North
1♠	3♠
4♠	End

'How did they manage to stay out of game?'

'I'm afraid North only raised to two spades at our table.'

'Two spades? With four-card support and two aces?'

'I know — he muttered something about nine losers. Anyway, John did his best by protecting with three diamonds when two spades was passed round to him, but all North did was try three spades and that ended the auction.'

'Lucky so-and-so. Well, I suppose it worked for him this time.'

'How did the play go?'

'West led the ◇K, which I won. I couldn't think of anything very imaginative except possibly an elimination play if trumps were 2-2, so I played two top spades but West showed out on the second. I now ran the ♣J to East's king, but he continued with a third trump. What could I do? I just went one off.'

'I don't think drawing trumps was a very good idea. Surely it is better to lose some of the tricks you have to lose as quickly as possible. I wonder what would have happened if you had played a diamond back at trick two.'

'Nothing much I expect. East would throw a small heart and West would win. I guess he would probably continue with another diamond.'

'You're in with a chance now, I think.'

'What do you mean?'

'You ruff in hand and run the ♣J. East wins with the queen and plays something back, probably another club. You win the ace, cross to the ♡A, draw two rounds of trumps, ruff a club, ruff a diamond, and exit with a heart. West has to win and give you a ruff and discard for your tenth trick.'

'But … but … isn't that a bit double-dummy? It's all very well when you can see all four hands.'

'I don't think it is such an unlikely layout after trick one. East's ◇10 looks very much like a singleton or a doubleton, and you find out for sure when you play a diamond back at trick two. As soon as you know West has six diamonds, it becomes quite likely that he has only two hearts.'

'Surely this is playing for a misdefence. West ought to unblock the ♡Q under the ace.'

'It is not very easy for him at all, particularly as you have not let him know what your trump holding is. How is he to know that your hand is not ♠ A K 8 5 2 ♡ A K 10 ◇ J 6 ♣ J 10 6? Would you have played any differently? If he has doubletons in both majors perhaps he ought to get it right, but with a singleton spade it is not unreasonable to hope partner has a trump trick.'

'Oh, well, yet another solid contract bites the dust. I don't suppose it will be the last one either. What happened on Board 2?'

TOURNAMENT BRIDGE

*A*lthough bridge is one of the few games where novices may find themselves pitted against the expert, there are a number of tournaments where only the stronger players compete. In this last section, our reporters take a peep at the great and good in play and relate some of their triumphs and disasters. Both are on a grander scale than those you and I might experience — and will provide amusement as well as inspiration.

AUKENED!

BY TONY GORDON

The fourth European Mixed Championships, sponsored by *Philip Morris*, took place in Monte Carlo in March 1996. In the Teams event, Sabine Auken, second in the world in the latest women's ranking list, pulled off a coup to make her game contract on this hand from the fourth-round match between *Nippgen* (Germany) and *Koistinen* (Finland):

Dealer: West
Love All

```
                 ♠ J 7 5 3 2
                 ♡ Q 10 7 2
                 ◇ J
                 ♣ K Q 6
  ♠ K 9                        ♠ 6
  ♡ A 9            N           ♡ K 6 5 4 3
  ◇ K Q 9 6 5 4  W   E         ◇ 8 7 3
  ♣ A 10 3         S           ♣ 9 7 4 2
                 ♠ A Q 10 8 4
                 ♡ J 8
                 ◇ A 10 2
                 ♣ J 8 5
```

South	West	North	East
Auken		*Nippgen*	
	1NT	NB	2◇*
NB	2♡	NB	NB
2♠	NB	3♠	NB
4♠	End		

*Transfer to hearts

West led the ◇K against 4♠ and Sabine Auken won with the ◇A. With three top losers in the rounded suits, she had to avoid a trump loser, but West was marked with the guarded ♠K. However, with barely a pause for thought, she led a low spade from hand at trick two — and West *ducked!*

Who says the old tricks are not the best?

THE MINISTER AT THE HELM

BY PATRICK JOURDAIN

Following the quarter-finals of the 1995 Marlboro World Bridge Championships, held in Beijing, I was invited to field a team of journalists against a foursome which included Ding Guengang, a senior member of the Politburo, and his son Yu Cheng. I was warned that they were excellent players. Just how good is illustrated by the Minister himself *(board rotated)*:

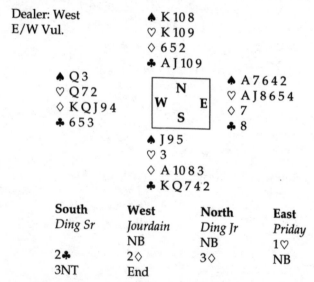

Dealer: West
E/W Vul.

North
♠ K 10 8
♡ K 10 9
◇ 6 5 2
♣ A J 10 9

West
♠ Q 3
♡ Q 7 2
◇ K Q J 9 4
♣ 6 5 3

East
♠ A 7 6 4 2
♡ A J 8 6 5 4
◇ 7
♣ 8

South
♠ J 9 5
♡ 3
◇ A 10 8 3
♣ K Q 7 4 2

South	West	North	East
Ding Sr	*Jourdain*	*Ding Jr*	*Priday*
	NB	NB	1♡
2♣	2◇	3◇	NB
3NT	End		

The 3◇ call by Ding Junior suggested that his father bid 3NT if he held a diamond stop, and the Minister obeyed, despite his singleton heart. Had I led my partner's suit, 3NT would have gone two light, but there would have been no story (at the other table East-West reached 4♡ and went two down). So I was lucky to make the wrong lead, the ◇K, and give Ding Senior the chance to show his great skill in the play.

Declarer gave the matter due thought. He then won the first diamond, giving the defence no chance to find the heart switch, and started on the clubs. Note that if declarer begins by running the ♠9, East will hold up. Declarer cannot play either major next because East will clear whichever major is played and have enough winners to beat the game when he gains the lead in the other major. As this article was submitted as a candidate for the *Bols* Bridge Press Prize, you may forgive a reference to the author's 1988 *Bols* Tip: 'In 3NT, with eight winners and five losers, play off your long suit.' Here declarer had only six winners, but playing off the clubs still worked.

East threw a heart on the second club, but on the third he had to give up a threat in one major. If he threw a spade, declarer could safely play on spades and use the fourth club later as an entry to play a heart to the ♡9. However, Priday correctly threw another heart. As declarer had only one heart, he could not yet begin the suit. On the fourth club, East threw another heart, but on the last he gave up a spade.

Now the Minister led the ♠9 and let it run. East ducked, and declarer followed with a *low* spade, fetching the queen, king, and ace. Priday cleared the spades, but declarer was now back in hand with the jack to lead a heart. It made no difference whether I played high or low. Priday could win only two hearts and the established spade (on which declarer threw his diamond) and then East had to concede the ninth trick to dummy's heart. Well played indeed!

After the diamond lead, the deal makes a fascinating double-dummy problem. We had another chance. When East is in with the ♠A, he must cash the ♡A and exit with a spade, leaving South locked in his own hand to concede diamonds to West.*

* *This article was one of the finalists in the 1995* Bols *Bridge Press Prize competition.*

SHINING STARS

BY BARRY RIGAL

One of the attractions of *The Macallan* Invitation Pairs, held annually in London, is the fact that the organisers invite crowd-pullers as well as World Champions. For the last two years, the largest crowds were drawn by Zia Mahmood— although it might conceivably have been something to do with the fact that his partner was Omar Sharif!

However, in 1996 the field was remarkably blessed with current world-title holders, as well as some of the stars from yesteryear. The American Bermuda Bowl team were there, together with Sabine Auken and Daniela von Arnim representing the Venice Cup holders, and the Hackett twins from the British World Junior Champions. The European Champions were represented by Lauria and Versace, and Sementa (playing with the great Pietro Forquet).

The hands which I have selected from the 1996 event feature the Bermuda Bowl winners in action, and the first two come from perhaps the least well-known pair in the current Bermuda Bowl winning team. Both Richard Freeman and Nick Nickell were playing in their first *Macallan*, and they naturally took a little time to acclimatise. However, they were soon up and running, on the following hand demonstrating the one legitimate way to beat the par contract:

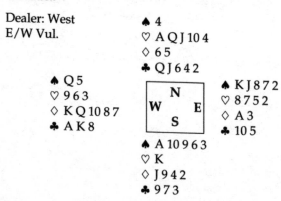

Dealer: West
E/W Vul.

```
                    ♠ 4
                    ♡ A Q J 10 4
                    ◇ 6 5
                    ♣ Q J 6 4 2
    ♠ Q 5                              ♠ K J 8 7 2
    ♡ 9 6 3            N              ♡ 8 7 5 2
    ◇ K Q 10 8 7    W     E           ◇ A 3
    ♣ A K 8            S              ♣ 10 5
                    ♠ A 10 9 6 3
                    ♡ K
                    ◇ J 9 4 2
                    ♣ 9 7 3
```

South	West	North	East
Versace	*Freeman*	*Lauria*	*Nickell*
	1◇	2NT*	NB
3♣	End		

*Hearts and clubs

Freeman led the ◇K; Nickell overtook and returned diamonds, allowing Freeman to play a third round of the suit; the best Versace could do was to ruff high, and cash two hearts to throw his last diamond. Then he crossed to the ♠A and led a trump. Freeman hopped up with the ♣K and played a fourth round of diamonds, promoting his partner's ♣10 for the setting trick.

My favourite declarer-play problem of the event came from the first round of the next day and was beautifully handled by Nick Nickell against Justin and Jason Hackett. It has an air of textbook about it, but one has to recognise the moment in real life too!

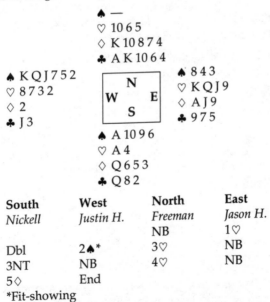

```
              ♠ —
              ♡ 10 6 5
              ◇ K 10 8 7 4
              ♣ A K 10 6 4
♠ K Q J 7 5 2      ┌─────┐      ♠ 8 4 3
♡ 8 7 3 2          │  N  │      ♡ K Q J 9
◇ 2            W   │     │  E   ◇ A J 9
♣ J 3              │  S  │      ♣ 9 7 5
                   └─────┘
              ♠ A 10 9 6
              ♡ A 4
              ◇ Q 6 5 3
              ♣ Q 8 2
```

South	West	North	East
Nickell	*Justin H.*	*Freeman*	*Jason H.*
		NB	1♡
Dbl	2♠*	3♡	NB
3NT	NB	4♡	NB
5◇	End		

*Fit-showing

Nickell received the lead of the ♠K; he carefully ruffed in dummy, and led a diamond to his queen; then he left trumps alone, and played off three rounds of clubs. Whether or not the third round was ruffed, he could ensure that he could lead the fourth round of clubs to discard his heart loser. As the cards lay, he could have played on trumps and survived, but his caution would have paid off if East had been 4-4-3-2.

When Bobby Wolff and Bob Hamman took on Jeff Meckstroth and Eric Rodwell on Vu-Graph, they edged them out, despite this missed opportunity for Bobby Wolff:

♠ Q 9
♡ J 9 6 5
◊ J 9 8
♣ J 8 7 2

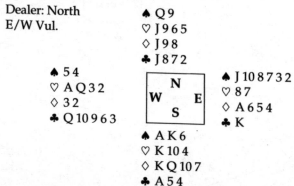

♠ A K 6
♡ K 10 4
◊ K Q 10 7
♣ A 5 4

You reach 3NT as South after East has shown a weak two bid in spades, and receive the lead of the ♣6. What would you play from dummy? If you play the ♣7, well done, East plays the ♣K. Which red suit is it right to play on?

All right, I admit it — that was a slightly tricky question; the key to the hand is to *duck* the first trick.

Dealer: North
E/W Vul.

♠ Q 9
♡ J 9 6 5
◊ J 9 8
♣ J 8 7 2

♠ 5 4
♡ A Q 3 2
◊ 3 2
♣ Q 10 9 6 3

N
W E
S

♠ J 10 8 7 3 2
♡ 8 7
◊ A 6 5 4
♣ K

♠ A K 6
♡ K 10 4
◊ K Q 10 7
♣ A 5 4

The right way to look at this hand, although by no means obvious at first or even second glance, is that if clubs are 4-2 you will need the heart finesse whether or not you duck the first trick. If clubs are 5-1, you gain a vital tempo by ducking the first trick, and unless West has all three key red-suit cards (in which case you have no chance anyway) you are safe.

EVERYBODY LOVES A BIG SWING

BY NIKOS SARANTAKOS

Bridge fans love them, bridge writers live from them, bridge players try to engineer them — or to avoid them. A good swing is in every player's mind, and double-figure swings can decide the fate of a match.

Swings come in every size and some are bigger than others. Under the current scale, the maximum you can gain or lose on any one board is 24 IMPs. This is not an everyday occurrence, though.

In the quarter-finals of the 1995 Bermuda Bowl and Venice Cup, played in Beijing, the following cute little deal generated some pretty large swings:

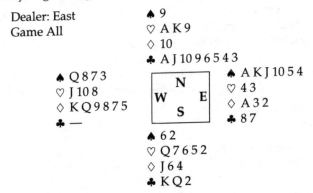

Dealer: East
Game All

```
              ♠ 9
              ♡ A K 9
              ◇ 10
              ♣ A J 10 9 6 5 4 3
♠ Q 8 7 3            ┌─────┐            ♠ A K J 10 5 4
♡ J 10 8            │  N  │            ♡ 4 3
◇ K Q 9 8 7 5    W │     │ E         ◇ A 3 2
♣ —               │  S  │            ♣ 8 7
                  └─────┘
              ♠ 6 2
              ♡ Q 7 6 5 2
              ◇ J 6 4
              ♣ K Q 2
```

The biggest swing recorded occurred in the Canada vs South Africa match, when the Canadians made 6♠ with one overtrick in one room and 6♣ doubled in the other. Both contracts had top losers, obviously, but the defenders failed to cash their tricks while it was still possible: South did not lead a heart against 6♠, while East tried to cash a second spade against 6♣. The outcome was that Canada gained no fewer than 3,000 points, or 22 IMPs!

Big deal, you'll say — after all, the fact that slams can produce large swings is not an earth-shattering discovery. Granted. What about non-slam swings? I cannot offer you a size 22, but if you are content with 21 then an example exists.

The biggest penalty in a Bermuda Bowl match occurred in the 1987 semi-finals. This was the fateful Board 71:

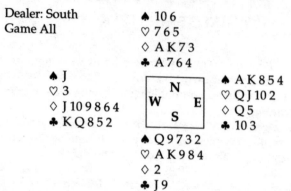

Dealer: South
Game All

North
♠ 10 6
♡ 7 6 5
◇ A K 7 3
♣ A 7 6 4

West
♠ J
♡ 3
◇ J 10 9 8 6 4
♣ K Q 8 5 2

East
♠ A K 8 5 4
♡ Q J 10 2
◇ Q 5
♣ 10 3

South
♠ Q 9 7 3 2
♡ A K 9 8 4
◇ 2
♣ J 9

The deal does not seem to contain great potential for swings; well, if North-South bid the heart game, they are likely to go down, possibly doubled, and this is what happened in the match between the USA and Taipei, when the USA gained 9 IMPs for making 2♡ plus two in one room and setting 4♡ doubled in the other.

The drama was in the other match, between Sweden and Great Britain, though not in the Closed Room where the late Jeremy Flint made a peaceful 3◇. This was the auction in the Open Room:

South	West	North	East
Armstrong	*Fallenius*	*Forrester*	*Lindqvist*
2NT (a)	NB	3♡ (b)	NB
NB	3NT (c)	Dbl	NB (d)
NB	Redbl (e)	NB	NB (f)
NB			

(a) Showing a two-suiter (without clubs) and 7-10 points
(b) Pass or correct
(c) For the minors
(d) No preference
(e) Playing with fire
(f) Getting burned!

Obviously, both Lindqvist and Fallenius could have avoided the disaster in one way or another, but the fact is that they played in 3NT redoubled, going no fewer than five down. The penalty was 2,800 points — a cool 21-IMP swing.

After that devastating blow to their morale, the Swedish team could not recover, and they eventually lost the match by 47 IMPs.

Some readers may remember one of S.J. Simon's stories, when a similar redouble is passed by partner. I hasten to add that the Swedish pair bear no resemblance to their fictional counterparts, even if they were both experts and unlucky — at least on that board.

However, the fact remains that lesser mortals do not have the potential to generate such a swing on this deal: they usually do not use double-edged gadgets, nor do they have such confidence in partner as to make, and then stand, such non-business redoubles!

Cartoon Corner

I MUST tell you about a hand!

NOT ENOUGH FOR A GAME TRY

BY JACK KROES

The following hand from the national team championship was reported in the official magazine of the Dutch Bridge Federation:

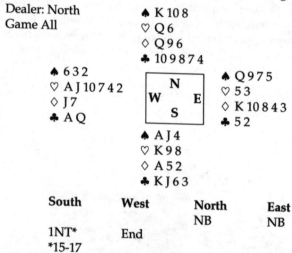

Dealer: North
Game All

```
                    ♠ K 10 8
                    ♡ Q 6
                    ◇ Q 9 6
                    ♣ 10 9 8 7 4
   ♠ 6 3 2                          ♠ Q 9 7 5
   ♡ A J 10 7 4 2      N            ♡ 5 3
   ◇ J 7            W     E         ◇ K 10 8 4 3
   ♣ A Q              S             ♣ 5 2
                    ♠ A J 4
                    ♡ K 9 8
                    ◇ A 5 2
                    ♣ K J 6 3
```

South	West	North	East
		NB	NB
1NT*	End		
*15-17			

West's remarkable pass was based on the fact that he had a good defence against 1NT.

After the lead of the ♡J, North put down his dummy, mumbling that his hand was really not good enough for a game try. South won the trick with the ♡Q and then played a low club to ♣J and ♣Q. West now switched to a beautiful card: the ◇J, covered by ◇Q and ◇K, and taken with the ace by declarer, who next led a club to West's ace. The ◇7 was returned; declarer tried dummy's ◇9, but alas! the remainder of the tricks went to the defence for five down.

'You were right, partner,' commented South drily, 'your hand was not good enough for a game try.'

TOLLE FINAL 1996

BY BOB ROWLANDS

The 1996 final of the annual inter-county event for teams of eight was as usual very keenly contested. Surprising absentees were Kent and Manchester, while the North-East were making their first appearance in this final for twenty-one years.

Merseyside & Cheshire went into an early lead with a 20-0 win over the North-East, but by the end of play on Saturday evening Surrey had taken a narrow lead with 51 VPs out of 80, with Cambs & Hunts, London, Sussex, and Middlesex close behind. Surrey (my team) were then heavily defeated by Sussex in the first match on Sunday.

Sandra Landy and John Elliott found a good defence on the deal below, and gave declarer a problem which he did not solve:

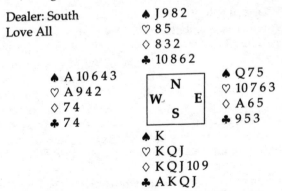

```
Dealer: South          ♠ J 9 8 2
Love All               ♡ 8 5
                       ♢ 8 3 2
                       ♣ 10 8 6 2
        ♠ A 10 6 4 3           ♠ Q 7 5
        ♡ A 9 4 2       N      ♡ 10 7 6 3
        ♢ 7 4       W       E  ♢ A 6 5
        ♣ 7 4           S      ♣ 9 5 3
                       ♠ K
                       ♡ K Q J
                       ♢ K Q J 10 9
                       ♣ A K Q J
```

Against 3NT, Elliott led the ♠4 to ♠8, ♠5, and ♠K. Declarer led the ♢K, won by East who returned the ♠7 to West's ♠A, and West continued with the ♠3. After much thought, declarer misguessed putting up the ♠J to go two down.

Good defence — but perhaps declarer should have reflected that with ♠Q-7-5 it was natural for East to play low at trick one, whereas with ♠10-7-5 East would probably have covered the ♠8.

There was plenty of action on the following:

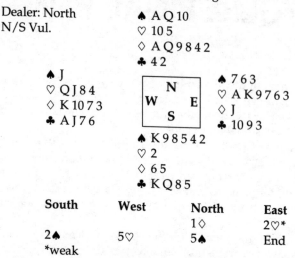

Dealer: North
N/S Vul.

North
♠ A Q 10
♡ 10 5
◇ A Q 9 8 4 2
♣ 4 2

West
♠ J
♡ Q J 8 4
◇ K 10 7 3
♣ A J 7 6

East
♠ 7 6 3
♡ A K 9 7 6 3
◇ J
♣ 10 9 3

South
♠ K 9 8 5 4 2
♡ 2
◇ 6 5
♣ K Q 8 5

South	West	North	East
		1◇	2♡*
2♠	5♡	5♠	End
*weak			

West led the ♡Q to ♡5, ♡K, and ♡3. Fearful of the diamonds, East rather naturally returned a club, the ♣10 to ♣K, ♣A, and ♣2, and West after some thought exited with ♠J. As this could hardly be from ♠J-x-x, it was apparent that West had length in both minors, so it would not be possible to establish the diamonds and draw trumps ending in dummy.

As declarer, I therefore ruffed one club in dummy and ran off the trumps hoping to squeeze West in the minors. This duly worked, but with Landy-Elliott being allowed to play in 4♡, and our result being duplicated at another table, we lost points on this board as well.

Sussex beat Surrey 19-1, and London also had a big win. With only two matches left, to have any chance Surrey needed a big win over London, but it was not to be and we were defeated 12-8.

Peter Crouch showed excellent technique on the following part-score deal against Peter Lee and myself:

Dealer: North
N/S Vul.

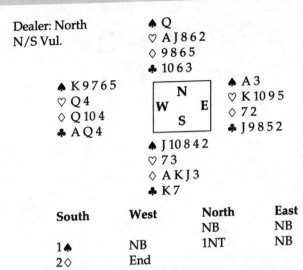

♠ Q
♡ A J 8 6 2
◇ 9 8 6 5
♣ 10 6 3

♠ K 9 7 6 5
♡ Q 4
◇ Q 10 4
♣ A Q 4

♠ A 3
♡ K 10 9 5
◇ 7 2
♣ J 9 8 5 2

♠ J 10 8 4 2
♡ 7 3
◇ A K J 3
♣ K 7

South	West	North	East
		NB	NB
1♠	NB	1NT	NB
2◇	End		

West led the ♡Q which was allowed to win. Declarer won the second trick with ♡A and led the ♠Q, won by East who returned the ◇2 to ◇A, ◇4, and ◇5. Declarer now led the ♠J; West played low (covering makes no difference), so declarer discarded the ♣3 and continued with the ♠4, ruffing with the ◇8. Resisting any temptation to play a club towards his king, Crouch now ruffed a heart with the ◇3, overruffed by West who returned the ◇Q won by declarer's ◇K.

In full control now, declarer ruffed a spade, ruffed a heart, and exited with a spade forcing West to lead a club at trick twelve. With all the other North-South pairs failing to register a plus score in our match, the points which London gained on this innocuous part-score because of Crouch's excellent play were more than London's eventual winning margin over Surrey.

With Sussex losing 20-0 to Middlesex, London's 12-8 win gave them a 4-VP lead over Cambs & Hunts with one match to go. The latter did well beating Sussex 17-3, but London defeated Hants & I.o.W. 20-0 to win overall by 7 VPs.

A PROFITABLE WEEKEND

BY DEREK RIMINGTON

In the late seventies the *Caransa-Philip Morris* International Bridge Tournament for teams was held annually in the Hilton Hotel, Amsterdam. It was a weekend not to be missed, especially if one could get a sponsor.

There was also a valuable prize awarded by the *ABN Bank* for the best-played hand. Here is the 1979 winner:

Dealer: West
Love All

```
                    ♠ A 7 5 3
                    ♡ A K
                    ◇ Q 9 7 3 2
                    ♣ 9 3
    ♠ Q J 8 4 2                       ♠ 9 6
    ♡ 7 3          ┌─────────┐        ♡ Q J 4
    ◇ J 10 8 6     │    N    │        ◇ K 4
    ♣ 7 4          │ W     E │        ♣ K Q J 10 6 5
                   │    S    │
                   └─────────┘
                    ♠ K 10
                    ♡ 10 9 8 6 5 2
                    ◇ A 5
                    ♣ A 8 2
```

South	West	North	East
	NB	1◇	2♣
Dbl	NB	2◇	NB
3♡	NB	3♠	NB
4♡	End		

Declarer was Wagenvoord of the Netherlands. His double showed values, not necessarily clubs. West led the ♣7.

Declarer won East's ♣10 with the ace, and immediately cashed the ♡A-K. The declarer then set up a possible endplay position by leading the ♣9. East won and cashed another high club. The fourth round of clubs was ruffed by declarer, who then exited with the ♡10. East won and played yet another club.

This was ruffed and this was the five-card ending:

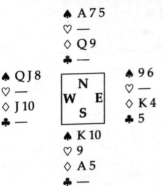

```
              ♠ A 7 5
              ♡ —
              ◇ Q 9
              ♣ —
♠ Q J 8                      ♠ 9 6
♡ —        ┌─────────┐       ♡ —
◇ J 10     │   N     │       ◇ K 4
♣ —        │ W   E   │       ♣ 5
           │   S     │
           └─────────┘
              ♠ K 10
              ♡ 9
              ◇ A 5
              ♣ —
```

On the ♡9, West had to discard a diamond. Dummy's ♠5 was discarded — its work having been accomplished.

The ♠10 was the entry to dummy, and the ◇Q was led setting up the ◇9 by force.

Cartoon Corner

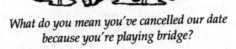

What do you mean you've cancelled our date because you're playing bridge?

AN IMAGINATIVE PSEUDO-COUP

BY ALAN TRUSCOTT

When the 1990 World Bridge Championships were held in Geneva, the Soviet Union had only recently become a fully-fledged member of the World Bridge Federation. Three teams — one from Moscow and two Moscow-Baltic combinations — were competing in the Louis Vuitton Teams Championships.

The Moscow players, Michael Rozenblum and Tim Zlotow, had a bidding misunderstanding on the diagrammed deal, but an imaginative pseudo-coup saved the day!

Dealer: North
Game All

```
                    ♠ 3 2
                    ♡ A Q J
                    ◇ J 10 6 5
                    ♣ A K J 6
  ♠ K 10 9                        ♠ A 7 4
  ♡ 10 8 7        ┌─────────┐     ♡ 9 6 5 3 2
  ◇ 9 2          │    N    │      ◇ Q 8 7
  ♣ Q 9 4 3 2    │ W     E │      ♣ 10 7
                 │    S    │
                 └─────────┘
                    ♠ Q J 8 6 5
                    ♡ K 4
                    ◇ A K 4 3
                    ♣ 8 5
```

South	West	North	East
		1NT	NB
2◇	NB	2NT	NB
3♣	Dbl	Redbl	NB
3♡	NB	4♣	NB
5♠	End		

One would expect North-South to reach 3NT, but there was a slight misunderstanding. The 2◇ bid was a strong Stayman, and 3♣ asked for further description. North's redouble was intended to show strong clubs, and North-South would presumably have made an overtrick if the bidding had ended.

Unfortunately, South believed that the redouble pinpointed a 3-3-3-4 distribution, and he charged on with an asking bid in hearts. 5♠ was much too high, needing, as a minimum, an even trump split with at least one top honour in the East hand.

The opening lead was the ◊9, won in dummy with the ◊10. A spade to the queen lost to the king, and a second diamond went to the ace. South took two rounds of hearts, ending in dummy in this position:

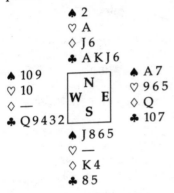

```
              ♠ 2
              ♡ A
              ◊ J 6
              ♣ A K J 6
♠ 10 9                    ♠ A 7
♡ 10      ┌─────────┐     ♡ 9 6 5
◊ —       │    N    │     ◊ Q
♣ Q9432   │  W   E  │     ♣ 10 7
          │    S    │
          └─────────┘
              ♠ J 8 6 5
              ♡ —
              ◊ K 4
              ♣ 8 5
```

Zlotow knew he had no chance, for East was about to take the ♠A and give his partner a diamond ruff. But he brought off a strange swindle.

He cashed dummy's ♡A and discarded, *mirabile dictu*, the ◊K. Then he led the spade from dummy and East did not feel inclined to rise with the ace — from his angle partner might have begun with ♠K-10 doubleton.

The ♠J won in the closed hand, and a third trump was led. East was now convinced that the remaining diamond was in his partner's hand. Without stopping to consider that there was no hope for the defence if that were true, he led a heart. South happily ruffed and eventually finessed in clubs to dispose of his diamond loser.

A DREAM COME TRUE

BY SVEND NOVRUP

For years I had been dreaming about organising an international pairs event along the lines of *The Macallan* in London but, as there is no Danish tradition for that sort of event, I had little hope of realising my dream.

In 1995, however, the newspaper for which I write the chess and bridge column finally gave in to my pleas and put up a DKR 100,000 prize fund. Thus, with the cooperation of the Danish Bridge Federation and the Phoenix Hotel Copenhagen, my dream came true and the first *Politiken* World Pairs took place in November.

The event was a Danish bridge celebration, with huge media coverage. Spectators flocked to watch twelve of the world's best pairs and four strong Danish pairs do battle in their tuxedos — the biggest crowds congregating around Omar Sharif's table. A tense, but always sporting, atmosphere characterised the event.

A first-time partnership of Zia Mahmood (Pakistan) and Peter Weichsel (US) won comfortably. They played a colourful — yet very solid — game, but Zia had one nasty moment sitting West against Geir Helgemo and Tor Helness of Norway:

```
Dealer: South          ♠ K Q 10 3
E/W Vul.               ♡ A Q 8 5
                       ◇ A 2
                       ♣ K Q 9

    ♠ A J 6 4                        ♠ 8 7 5
    ♡ —            N                 ♡ 9 7
    ◇ K 7 6 5 3  W   E               ◇ Q J 10 9 8
    ♣ A J 5 3        S               ♣ 10 7 4

                       ♠ 9 2
                       ♡ K J 10 6 4 3 2
                       ◇ 4
                       ♣ 8 6 2
```

South	West	North	East
4♡	Dbl	Redbl	End

Zia had to double — but the redouble told him that he had not taken a winning action. South made eleven easy tricks for +1080. It would have been cheaper for East-West to run to 5◊, but neither of them is known for ducking a challenge.

Weichsel was one of the heroes in the best hand of the event, where he overcalled East's opening 1♠ bid with 5♣ and played there against a spade lead:

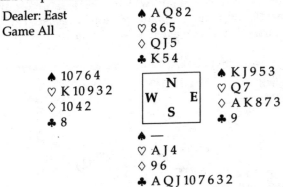

Dealer: East
Game All

♠ A Q 8 2
♡ 8 6 5
◊ Q J 5
♣ K 5 4

♠ 10 7 6 4
♡ K 10 9 3 2
◊ 10 4 2
♣ 8

N
W　　E
S

♠ K J 9 5 3
♡ Q 7
◊ A K 8 7 3
♣ 9

♠ —
♡ A J 4
◊ 9 6
♣ A Q J 10 7 6 3 2

Weichsel played low from dummy and ruffed in hand. He drew trumps with the ♣Q, advanced the ◊9 — and let it run when West unsuspectingly played low. East had to win, and fired back the ♡Q which Weichsel won to enter dummy with the ♣6 to ♣K. He discarded a diamond on the ♠A and ran the ◊Q, pitching a heart when East did not cover — eleven tricks made.

　　Defending against the same contract, Dave Berkowitz of the US made the same lead. Dennis Koch-Palmund of Denmark won in dummy, pitching a diamond, and then led a low diamond putting a lot of pressure on Larry Cohen, East. The American thought for a long time, but finally ducked. Berkowitz won with his ◊10 and returned a spade, which was ruffed high in hand. Declarer entered dummy with a middle trump, ruffed a diamond high, crossed to the ♣5, and ruffed the last diamond high. Then came the ♡A, on which Cohen unblocked the ♡Q, followed by a low heart. A second deadly trap was avoided when Berkowitz won the trick with the ♡9 instead of a 'crocodile' ♡K, trusting Cohen to play the ♡J first from ♡Q-J doubleton in order to avoid disaster!

　　It was brilliant declarer play at both tables — even though only one South succeeded.

A LITTLE LUCK

BY GEIR HELGEMO

The *Cap Volmac*, held in The Hague, is an invitation pairs tournament scored in IMPs in which concentration and the ability to read the opponents' minds are sorely tested. The two hands below are from the 1996 event, which I won with my partner Tor Helness.

On this deal we were pitted against a very strong French pair:

Dealer: North
E/W Vul.

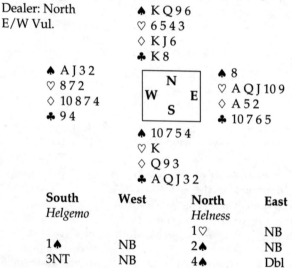

♠ KQ96
♡ 6543
◇ KJ6
♣ K8

♠ AJ32
♡ 872
◇ 10874
♣ 94

♠ 8
♡ AQJ109
◇ A52
♣ 10765

♠ 10754
♡ K
◇ Q93
♣ AQJ32

South	West	North	East
Helgemo		*Helness*	
		1♡	NB
1♠	NB	2♠	NB
3NT	NB	4♠	Dbl
End			

I was sitting South and when dummy appeared after the ♣9 lead, I was almost certain that East had doubled on a heart stack and short spades. I won in hand and when a spade to the king dropped East's ♠8 I knew West had the rest of the trumps. I now cashed the ♣K and then played the ◇K, which held. Another diamond was won by East, who continued with ace and another heart. I ruffed, and started playing high clubs through West, who had no answer. East-West got their aces for a score of minus 590 and a loss of 11 IMPs. Without the double, the contract would probably have failed.

To win the *Cap Volmac* you need a little luck. Here we capitalised on a rare declarer error:

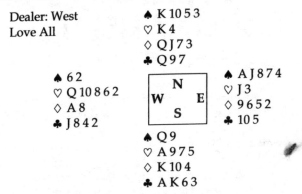

Dealer: West
Love All

♠ K 10 5 3
♡ K 4
◇ Q J 7 3
♣ Q 9 7

♠ 6 2
♡ Q 10 8 6 2
◇ A 8
♣ J 8 4 2

♠ A J 8 7 4
♡ J 3
◇ 9 6 5 2
♣ 10 5

♠ Q 9
♡ A 9 7 5
◇ K 10 4
♣ A K 6 3

Helness in the West seat opened a weak 2♡. After two passes, South bid 2NT and was raised to 3NT by North.

Helness led a low heart, and South made a mistake by calling for the ♡K from dummy. I played the ♡J to unblock the suit.

Now South had to guess which ace Helness held. He misguessed and led a spade from dummy, which I promptly took with my ace to play my second and last heart for one down and a 10-IMP pick up.

South should have played low on the heart lead, but everybody makes mistakes — even in this quality event.

RULING THE GAME WITH GOLDWATER

The late Harry Goldwater, one of the USA's leading Tournament Directors, approached his duties with a unique sense of humour. On one occasion he was called to rule after a player had doubled a 2♡ bid that no-one had made, and the following dialogue took place:

Player: 'I must have heard it from another table.'

Harry: 'Well then, why don't you take your cards over to the other table and see if you can beat it?'

From the Atlanta Nationals Bulletin

GETTING ACCLIMATISED

BY TOM TOWNSEND

W e travelled to Semerang, on the North coast of Java, to play in the 26th Djarum Cup for international teams by invitation of the sponsors, the country's leading cigarette company.

There are some good players in Indonesia: reaching the last eight of the 1995 Bermuda Bowl was just one of many strong performances over the years, and the distinctive local style of overbidding, backed up with fine card-play, is tough to play against. If your defence is inaccurate, you're in for a rough ride, and when the cards lie well, this approach is virtually unbeatable. This is a prime example from the Swiss Teams qualifying stage:

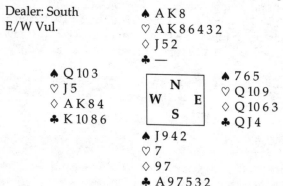

Dealer: South
E/W Vul.

North:
♠ A K 8
♡ A K 8 6 4 3 2
♢ J 5 2
♣ —

West:
♠ Q 10 3
♡ J 5
♢ A K 8 4
♣ K 10 8 6

East:
♠ 7 6 5
♡ Q 10 9
♢ Q 10 6 3
♣ Q J 4

South:
♠ J 9 4 2
♡ 7
♢ 9 7
♣ A 9 7 5 3 2

Justin and Jason Hackett played in 4♡ as North-South, going one off on a misdefence. Les Steel and I were quietly satisfied with the auction at our table:

South	West	North	East
	Steel		*Townsend*
NB	1♦	Dbl	2♦
2♠	NB	3♦	NB
4♣	NB	4♡	Dbl
5♣	Dbl	5♠	Dbl
End			

North-South made other dubious bids, but I pin most of the blame on North's double. One-level doubles suggest tolerance for all unbid suits. Exceptions are best limited to when the hand is too strong for anything else, and when the doubler can control the auction — preferably both. A simple 1♡ may seem overweight, but it does say what the hand's about, and you can show extra strength later, which is a lot easier than denying what you have already advertised.

I doubled 4♡ 'on the bidding,' and would have got 300 had South not repeated clubs. He wasn't too pleased to be put back to 5♠, but we couldn't beat it. Declarer ruffed the third round of diamonds, played ♠J to the Queen and Ace, Ace and another heart *ruffed with the* ♠9, and drew trumps finessing the ♠8. Ruffing the heart low would have allowed Steel to withhold the ♠10, scotching the entry.

Back home such a fluke might call for embarrassed apologies, in the way that a tennis player raises his racquet to acknowledge a net-cord. In Indonesia bidding and making outrageous contracts is the best part of the game, and the kibitzers cheered appreciatively. Which was fine with us: the hand was well played, and the unashamed applause indicated that we were the team to beat. But we still needed a result or two to reach the all-play-all final, and these 'Indonesian games' were getting to us. Should we rely on the percentages to see us through, or bid 'em up ourselves, just to play on level terms?

We stuck to our normal game on the whole, but resolved borderline decisions aggressively. A few more nervous, close matches left us in need of a good last win. When we came through 81-11 IMPs up (the 11 being a vulnerable game which required several cards right, a couple of breaks, good play, and a misdefence) we were in the final, *and* acclimatised to Indonesian bridge.

We won by nearly a match.

Jason Hackett was a little sceptical as he sorted the freak North hand below: any 9-4 shape is a one in 100,000 shot. Then came the realisation that he had dealt it himself. North-South can make 7◊, and also 7NT — very relevant if East-West attempt to save for 1100 in 7♡.

Dealer: East
N/S Vul.

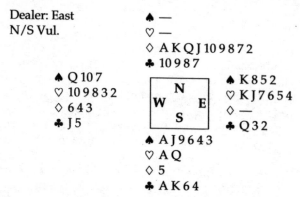

```
                          ♠ —
                          ♡ —
                          ◊ A K Q J 10 9 8 7 2
                          ♣ 10 9 8 7
  ♠ Q 10 7                                    ♠ K 8 5 2
  ♡ 10 9 8 3 2          N                      ♡ K J 7 6 5 4
  ◊ 6 4 3          W          E                ◊ —
  ♣ J 5                  S                      ♣ Q 3 2
                          ♠ A J 9 6 4 3
                          ♡ A Q
                          ◊ 5
                          ♣ A K 6 4
```

The Indonesian ladies got straight to the point with the sequence 1♣ (Precision) — 7◊! Both pairs in our match missed it in interesting fashion:

South	West	North	East
Justin H.		*Jason H.*	
			NB
1♠	NB	2◊	2♡
3♣	3♡	6◊	End

Not easy to bid nor adjudicate: Jason felt that 6◊ had been fairly descriptive; Justin obviously did not, and suggested a forcing 4◊ instead.

At our table the bidding went:

South	West	North	East
	Townsend		*Steel*
			1♡
Dbl	1NT (!)	5◊ (!)	NB
6◊	End		

North was 'sandbagging' with his apparently feeble 5◊. He could read my 1NT as a bluff, and hoped to be pushed to 6◊ and make it doubled. But not re-raising to seven was just plain wet.

214

NOT A GOOD START

BY MATTHEW GRANOVETTER

The annual festival in Tel Aviv is my favourite tournament. In 1996 players from more than twenty countries took part, and we had the largest attendance ever, approximately 2,750 tables — but the highlight was when more than one hundred children, ages 7-12, marched into the hall to play their special event.

In the IMP Pairs the following deal was the highlight of the tournament for Tel Aviv's Rozy Bezner. Having immigrated from Milan twenty years ago, Bezner was not a little in awe of her Italian opponents, Pietro Forquet and Guido Ferraro. This was the first board:

Dealer: West
N/S Vul.

```
                        ♠ 4
                        ♡ A 5 3
                        ◇ Q J 10 4
                        ♣ K 10 8 7 5
    ♠ A K Q J 9 2                         ♠ 6 5 3
    ♡ K               ┌─────────┐         ♡ J 10 9 7 2
    ◇ 9 7 3 2         │    N    │         ◇ K 8 6
    ♣ Q 3             │ W     E │         ♣ 6 2
                      │    S    │
                      └─────────┘
                        ♠ 10 8 7
                        ♡ Q 8 6 4
                        ◇ A 5
                        ♣ A J 9 4
```

South	West	North	East
Bezner	Forquet	Granovetter	Ferraro
	1♠	Dbl	NB
2♠	3♠	NB	NB
4♡	NB	NB	Dbl
NB	NB	4♠	NB
5♣	NB	NB	Dbl
End			

Bezner had no problem in 5♣ after picking up the trumps and East had *linguini* on his face for doubling 4♡. There was a brief uproar in Italian among the players, summed up finally by Forquet in understated English: 'It's not a good start.'

HARD LOOKS, GOOD PLAYS

BY ALASDAIR FORBES

The Gold Cup is the most prestigious event for teams-of-four in the British bridge calendar, and as such it is seeded. A few years ago, however, two strong Scottish teams clashed in one of the early rounds; the crucial deal produced no swing, but it was pure theatre at the table where I was watching:

```
Dealer: South          ♠ A 8 4
Game All               ♡ 6
                       ◇ K Q J 10 3
                       ♣ A K J 9
   ♠ J 9 3                           ♠ Q 5
   ♡ 9 4 3          ┌─────────┐      ♡ Q 10 8 2
   ◇ 9 7 5 2        │    N    │      ◇ A 6
   ♣ Q 10 8       W │         │ E    ♣ 7 5 4 3 2
                    │    S    │
                    └─────────┘
                       ♠ K 10 7 6 2
                       ♡ A K J 7 5
                       ◇ 8 4
                       ♣ 6
```

This was the bidding in Room 1, where Derek Diamond and Victor Silverstone (for the Haase, Goldberg, Matheson, Silverstone and Diamond team) were North-South:

South	North
1♠	2◇
2♡	3♣
3♡	4NT
5◇	6NT

Twelve tricks were made for +1440.

In Room 2, where the North-South seats were occupied by Sandy Duncan and Douglas Piper (for the Duncan, Piper, Denoon and Sanders team) the auction went:

South	North
1♠	2◇
2♡	4NT
5◇	6♠

Victor Goldberg (West) took a few seconds to consider his lead and then produced a devilish ♣10. Sandy Duncan thanked partner automatically, and then gave that ♣10 a long, hard look. Goldberg looked straight at Duncan as if defying him to finesse the club at trick one and go down quickly. Declarer spent the next couple of minutes trying to find some other play that needed the doubleton Q-J of trumps, and eventually decided that Goldberg was quite capable of leading the ten from ♣Q-10-x or a similar holding. He called for the ♣J, which held, and Goldberg gave him another hard look.

There was still a lot of work to be done, and I am sure that Duncan thought that he was going down because he had to play two more rounds of clubs to discard his losing diamonds. It was quite likely that the third round would be ruffed, but he had no other option. When the third club stood up, he called for the ◇K; Matheson (East) covered, and Duncan ruffed.

At this point declarer looked years younger, and only had to play the trumps for one loser. This he achieved by playing the ♠K and ♠A, and then he ran the diamonds claiming twelve tricks for +1430.

Top players rarely say much after a hand like this, as they usually know that a diamond lead would beat the slam at trick one. The bidding, however, suggested a club lead, and indeed a club was led at the other table giving North an easy ride.

On this occasion Victor Goldberg smiled and nodded his approval of the play as he returned his cards to the board.

Although the board was flat, it helped Duncan's team to keep in touch, trailing by just a few IMPs on the set, and they went from strength to strength, eventually winning comfortably by over 20 IMPs. There is little doubt in my mind that had Duncan lost 17 IMPs on that deal, his team would have been playing 'catch-up' bridge — and we all know how difficult that can be.

BIG SESSION

BY BRIAN SENIOR

The first qualifying session for the Pairs event in the 1996 *Philip Morris* European Mixed Championships did not go well for top Israeli pair, David and Daniella Birman. The second session, however, was a different story as they powered their way to 65% and rose to ninth overall. Here are a couple of their better boards.

Dealer: East
E/W Vul.

```
                    ♠ 10 9 7 4
                    ♡ J 2
                    ♢ 8 5 4 2
                    ♣ A J 5
    ♠ 8 6 2              N            ♠ A K Q 3
    ♡ K 10 6 4       W     E         ♡ 9 7 3
    ♢ K 10 7            S            ♢ A Q J 6
    ♣ 10 7 3                          ♣ 9 4
                    ♠ J 5
                    ♡ A Q 8 5
                    ♢ 9 3
                    ♣ K Q 8 6 2
```

South	West	North	East
David B.		Daniella B.	
			1♣ (a)
2♣	Dbl (b)	3♣	End
(a) 16+			
(b) 5+			

West led the ♠6 and East won the queen and ace and then switched to the ♢Q followed by the ♢A and a third diamond. All the high cards were marked for Birman now and he ruffed the diamond and played a low heart from hand without pause for thought.

Now West might also have thought back to the bidding, and appreciated that partner must have a minimum hand to allow North-South to play in 3♣, hence it would be a good idea to go in with the ♡K. But West ducked without thought, and that was the contract. Plus 110 was an excellent score for North-South.

The key to the success of David Birman's play was that it was done so smoothly. Had he had to think about it, West would also have had time to think and would surely have got it right.

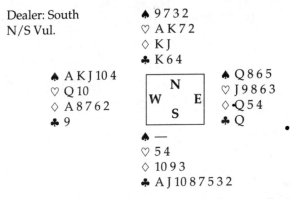

Dealer: South
N/S Vul.

North
♠ 9 7 3 2
♡ A K 7 2
◇ K J
♣ K 6 4

West
♠ A K J 10 4
♡ Q 10
◇ A 8 7 6 2
♣ 9

East
♠ Q 8 6 5
♡ J 9 8 6 3
◇ Q 5 4
♣ Q

South
♠ —
♡ 5 4
◇ 10 9 3
♣ A J 10 8 7 5 3 2

South	West	North	East
David B.	Gianardi	Daniella B.	De Falco
4♣	Dbl	Redbl	NB
NB	4◇	5♣	5◇
6♣	Dbl	End	

Not everyone can open 4♣, for systemic reasons, but here the natural opening was a big winner, putting West under pressure. Carla Gianardi doubled and Daniella Birman redoubled. When that came back round to her, Gianardi removed herself to 4◇; Daniella Birman bid 5♣ and Dano De Falco, with a useful hand in support of diamonds, bid 5◇. Now David Birman thought that he would not only be facing a good hand, but also diamond shortage, and bid 6♣.

Gianardi doubled and led a top spade, and must have felt ill when that got ruffed. Declarer drew trumps and led a diamond. He was always going to get the suit right after the auction, but a rattled West went up with the ace to save him any worries.

Plus 1540 earned, of course, a huge match-point score.

WHO'S WHO

Gustavu Aglione (a pseudonym) plays bridge in the Netherlands.

Simon Ainger writes for *Bridge Plus.*

Jimmy Allan has contributed to most major international magazines.

Len Armstrong contributes to *International Popular Bridge Monthly.*

Dr Ann Elisabeth Auhagen is a German Ladies International.

Dr Ulrich Auhagen, German International, is a Vu-Graph commentator and author of several books on bridge.

David Bird is Bridge Correspondent for *The Mail on Sunday* and the *London Evening Standard.* He has written some thirty books on bridge, including twenty with the late Terence Reese.

Richard Bird plays bridge in Oxfordshire.

Tim Bourke, Australian champion, writes for several international bridge magazines and is the author (together with David Bird) of *Tournament Acol.*

Mr Bridge is the UK distributor for *The Daily Bridge Calendar.* Enquiries welcome on 01483 489961.

Bernard Brighton runs bridge courses and holidays for beginners and intermediate players. Enquiries welcome on 01742 307555.

Sally Brock is a former Ladies World Champion, currently Assistant Editor of *Bridge Magazine.* Her latest book is *Step-by-step Overcalls.*

Alan A. Brown plays bridge in Berkshire.

Su Burn, English International, is a bridge journalist.

Stephen Cashmore writes for several English bridge magazines.

Ralph Churney, English International, plays bridge in Liverpool.

Eric Crowhurst, English International, is the author of *Precision Bidding in Acol* and *Acol in Competition*, and writes for many leading magazines and newspapers world-wide.

Nevena Deleva is a former Bulgarian European Champion, a bridge teacher, and professional player. Enquiries on 0115-942 2615.

Maureen Dennison is a former Ladies World Champion and a regular contributor to several international bridge magazines.

Peter Donovan is *The Daily Mail* Bridge Columnist.

Peter Dunn plays bridge in Northamptonshire.

Guy Dupont is one of the Editors of the French magazine *Le Bridgeur*.

Allan Falk of the USA is the author of *Spingold Challenge*.

Alasdair Forbes is the Editor of the *Scottish Bridge Union News* magazine.

Geoff Fogg plays bridge in Buckinghamshire.

Benito Garozzo, thirteen times World Champion, and a member of the legendary Italian *Blue Team*, is one of the all-time Greats.

Tony Gordon writes for *Bridge Plus*.

Matthew Granovetter, US International, is the Editor, together with his wife Pamela, of *Bridge Today*.

Nigel Guthrie writes for *Bridge Plus*.

Paul Hackett, British International, is a bridge professional.

Peter Hawkes writes for *Bridge Plus*.

Amanda Hawthorn is a bridge author and teacher who specialises in holiday courses for less-experienced players. Enquiries welcome on 01895 824230.

Geir Helgemo (age 26) is a Norwegian bridge professional and journalist. A former Junior Champion, he has won most of the world's important events, including the *Generali* Individual.

Alan Hiron, British International, is *The Independent* Bridge Columnist.

Edward Horsup plays and teaches bridge in Berkshire.

Mark Horton, British International, is the Editor of *Bridge Magazine*.

Audrey Hoffman is a bridge professional.

Martin Hoffman is a bridge professional and author of several bridge books including *On the Other Hand*.

Dave Huggett is one of England's leading players and teachers, and writes for *Bridge Plus*.

Sid Ismail plays and teaches bridge in South Africa.

Patrick Jourdain is the Bridge Correspondent of *The Daily Telegraph* and Principal of the Cardiff School of Bridge.

Andrew Kambites is the author of several books, the most recent of which is *Guide to Better Acol Bridge* (with Ron Klinger).

Chris Kinloch plays bridge in the south of England.

Phillip King, British International, is the author with his father Robert of *The Kings' Tales*, *Contract Killers*, and *Farewell, My Dummy!*

Ron Klinger, Australian International, is one of the world's leading bridge writers. His most recent books include *Power Acol*.

Jack Kroes is a Dutch bridge journalist.

Mike Lawrence, US International and one of the original *Aces*, is a leading bridge writer and professional.

Peter Littlewood is a leading Yorkshire player, a bridge journalist, and an acknowledged authority on bridge history.

Rodney McCombe plays bridge in Co. Down.

Bernard Magee is the bridge consultant for Mr Bridge and the author of the *Collins Bridge Quiz Book*.

Morag Malcolm, Scottish International, is a leading bridge teacher and administrator.

Paul Mendelson is a bridge consultant and the author of *100 Tips for Better Bridge*.

Sue Maxwell is a bridge teacher and the EBU's Press Officer.

Freddie North, British International, is a bridge professional and writer. His bridge books include *Conventional Bidding Explained*.

Svend Novrup is the Bridge Columnist of Danish national newspaper *Politiken*.

Tony Parkinson plays bridge in Berkshire.

David Parry is *The European* Bridge Columnist and teaches bridge in London. Enquiries on 0181-749 4352.

Barrie Partridge is the Editor of the *Sheffield Bridge Club Newsletter*.

Queenie Penguin, Antarctic International, writes for *Bridge Plus*.

David Perkins plays bridge in Buckinghamshire.

Bob Pitts writes the bridge column for the *Liverpool Daily Post*.

Tony Priday, former British European Champion, is the Bridge Columnist of *The Sunday Telegraph* .

Hilary Quintana (a pseudonym) plays bridge in Hampshire.

Terence Reese (d. 1996), British World Champion, was the world's leading bridge writer.

Barry Rigal is the author of *Step-by-Step: Deceptive Declarer Play* and a leading bridge analyst, journalist and Vu-Graph commentator.

Derek Rimington, British International, writes for *The Field* and contributes to most leading bridge magazines.

Andrew Robson, former European and Junior World Champion, is a bridge professional and author, and *The Spectator* Bridge Columnist.

Danny Roth is a bridge professional and teacher. His books include *The Expert Improver*. Enquiries on 0181-997 2970.

Ken Rowe is the Editor of *English Bridge*.

Bob Rowlands, British International, writes for several magazines and teaches bridge in London. Enquiries on 0171-385 0933.

Nikos Sarantakos lives in Luxemburg and has contributed articles to various European and US magazines.

P.F. Saunders (d. 1996) was a leading writer of humorous bridge fiction.

Erwin Schön is an Austrian bridge teacher and journalist.

Brian Senior, British International, is the Editor of *International Popular Bridge Monthly*. His books include *Raising Partner*.

Robert Sheehan is a British International and *The Times* Bridge Columnist.

Marc Smith, English International, writes for several bridge magazines.

Malcolm Simpson plays and teaches bridge in Oxfordshire.

Warner Solomon plays bridge in Devon.

Les Steel, British International, has some thirty Scottish caps to his credit.

Mike Swanson is the Tournament Director for *Diamond Bridge*. Holiday enquiries welcome on 01922 26017.

Kitty Teltscher plays bridge in London.

Tom Townsend is a Junior World Champion and a bridge professional. Enquiries on 0118-978 1875.

Alan Truscott, former European Champion and US International, is *The New York Times* Bridge Columnist.

Neil Ward cannot play bridge!

Peter Waterman plays bridge in Yorkshire.

Richard Wheen composes double dummy problems for *Bridge Plus*.

Mike Whittaker is the author, together with Bob Rowlands and Amanda Hawthorn, of *Test Your Acol Bidding*.

Elena Jeronimidis is the Bridge Columnist of *Teletext on 4* and the Editor of *Bridge Plus*, the monthly bridge magazine available by subscription @ £26.75 for 12 monthly issues from PO Box 384, Reading RG1 5YP (telephone /fax 0118-935 1052).